SUPERPOWER INVESTING

SUPERPOWER INVESTING

The Superpower Way to Bank
and Invest Your Money
(Featuring the Revolutionary
New Investment Discovery
SYNCHROVEST)

by
Robert Lichello

FARNSWORTH PUBLISHING CO., INC.
Rockville Centre, New York 11570

Second Printing.
Library of Congress Catalog Card No. 74-78729.
ISBN 087-8630-422.
Manufactured in the United States of America.

For Nancy

The author is indebted to the Rowe Price New Horizons Fund, Inc. for graciously supplying him historical data through the years required to prepare this book; to the New York Stock Exchange and Dow Jones & Company, Inc. for similar services; to Harper & Row, Publishers, Inc., for permission to quote from *Yankee Genius,* by Earl L. Smith; and to Johnson's Charts Inc., for permission to reprint the Dollar Cost Average table that appeared originally in Johnson's Investment Company Charts, 1958 edition.

"That which rules within, when it is according to nature, is so affected with respect to the events which happen, that it always easily adapts itself to that which is possible and is presented to it. For it requires no definite material, but it moves toward its purpose, under certain conditions however; and it makes a material for itself out of that which opposes it, as fire lays hold of what falls into it, by which a small light would have been extinguished: but when the fire is strong, it soon appropriates to itself the matter which is heaped on it, and consumes it, and rises higher by means of this very material . . .

"Everything harmonizes with me, which is harmonious to thee, O Universe. Nothing for me is too early nor too late, which is due time for thee. Everything is fruit to me which thy seasons bring, O Nature . . ."

—Marcus Aurelius, *Meditations*

Contents

Preface

You are about to read what the author believes to be a most unusual financial book. Like many of you, he, too, has read with much pleasure—if not profit—the myriad "How-To" books that purport to light our way to the Promised Land of plenty. And, like many of you, he has eagerly attempted to apply some of these techniques during the course of his own investment internship.

But a funny thing seems to happen on the way to the market. Nothing works the way it was supposed to work. Brokers chuckle maliciously as they divine your purpose (they can tell which book you've read by the kind of order you give them), but you push doggedly on, convinced there has been a giant conspiracy all along to prevent your success and that, now that you *know*, you are going to make monkeys out of the whole lot. Alas, when the ticker tape stutters to a stop and you stare in disbelief at the final lapidary legends inscribed thereon, you realize who the monkey is.

The techniques fail for a variety of reasons. Sometimes they carry within them the seeds of their own destruction. They may work for a few people, but collapse under the weight of the mob. They may work under a given set of circumstances, but not under others. They may work for investors with one kind of temperament, but not for investors temperamentally opposed. Doubtless, the authors were all sincere; but doubtless, too, the likelihood that luck played a major role in the majority of these success stories.

It is all part of the Money Myth, whose origins stretch back to the primal scream, "I wish I were rich and didn't have to worry about money!" Two incidents recently witnessed serve to reveal the tainted heritage of our Money Myth. In the first, a woman shopper at the supermarket check-out counter abruptly challenged the clerk's computation with: "You charged me 34 cents for a head of lettuce. I believe the price is 33 cents." The clerk, fresh out of high school, laughed scornfully as she handed her the coin. "It's only a penny."

"Young lady, only poor people don't care about pennies," she replied crushingly, "and I'm not poor."

She wasn't, either. Outside, she climbed into a Mercedes.

A few months later a slovenly young man was observed purchasing a package of cigarettes in a grocery store. "You forgot your penny change," the clerk said.

"Keep it," said the young man grandly. "I don't want to carry those things around."

He left the store, climbed into a ten-year-old junkyard reject and clattered away smokily.

According to the Money Myth, the lady must have got rich by being a tightwad. That may have helped, but she was a tightwad *because* she was rich. And because she wanted to stay that way.

In supermarkets, you will see that the most careless shoppers are generally the shabbiest dressed, while those who are obviously more affluent patiently compare the values and often read the labels to determine which brands contain the fewest—or least carcinogenic—poisons, thus to live long enough to enjoy their money and, incidentally, to save on medical bills. To the middle class, thrift means protection against a rainy day. To the rich, it means guaranteed sunshine. There's a world of difference in the two viewpoints. True security, said Joseph Wood Krutch, lies not in the things one has, but in the things one can do without.

Another branch of the Myth family worships a household god called What's the Use?, a deity represented by a slouched and hopeless figure with his hands in his pockets. Members of this religion believe that if you're poor, you'll stay poor, and that you can't turn a penny into a dollar. And yet it was the author's pleasure some years ago to discuss finance with a rather remarkable old gentleman on Welfare. He looked like a Welfare client and he lived like a Welfare client—but by saving nickels and dimes out of his $71-a-month relief check, he had painstakingly managed to accumulate $21,000 worth of stock in the dream of becoming self-sufficient and making his own way in life!

Why is *Superpower Investing* an "unusual financial book"? Because we believe it will work for you, and you, and you. Its success does not depend upon luck, circumstance, a temporary loophole, time and study, financial savvy, inside information, or judgment. It worked yesterday, it works today, it will work tomorrow; and there is nothing anybody can do nor any rule that can be changed to prevent you from using it profitably, both to make money and—more important—to reduce your vulnerability to loss. The housewife with $50 a month to invest can now do just as well as the financial wizards with their millions—and probably better if they are not using SYNCHROVEST. And if a dollar value can be placed upon peace of mind, SYNCHROVEST can make each man a Croesus.

SYNCHROVEST was designed to conform with Nature's insistence upon balance, and in further pursuit of that goal, we have balanced our investment discoveries in this book with what we believe to be exciting and rewarding ideas concerning savings—without which there could be no investment. Together, they offer a well-rounded strategy for acquiring and preserving capital in these often bewildering and perilous times—and *enjoy* doing it!

And if, along the way, you see others grow greater in greener pastures, remember that they are being fatted for the slaughter; you are dieting for health.

The Wall Street Shell Game —Why You Keep Guessing Wrong 1

"HUGE PROFITS IN LOW PRICE STOCKS! Send $5 for list of three undervalued, overlooked stocks solidly based in space technology and poised for tremendous profits in the months to come....

"FORTUNES IN LIFE INSURANCE STOCKS! Only a handful of investors are aware of the fantastic fortunes that have been made—and will be made—in life insurance stocks. Do you know, for example, that $10,000 invested in five of America's best known insurance companies only ten years ago would today be worth $100,000? Send $10 for a selected list of nine insurance stocks that promise outstanding growth in the boom years ahead....

"CRASH COMING? Be prepared to protect yourself against severe losses and take advantage of golden buying opportunities in today's uncertain market. Send $15 for our report X-11-A just out entitled BOOM COMING? . . . .

" 'I WANNA MAKE A POTFUL OF DOUGH—QUICK!' Well, it's only natural to want to make a lot of money without having to wait around for it, but honestly, we don't know the answer. And we don't think anybody else does, either. Seriously, though, as a brokerage firm, we can buy and sell for you securities of good, solid companies in which you have the opportunity of investing in American industry and sharing in its prosperity . . . ."

Sound familiar? Recognize the pitch? If so, you're a battle-hardened vet with scars to prove it and you may sit in the front row of our class. Almost all of us know someone who is "in the market" and who talks knowingly of earnings' ratios, stock splits, rights, etc. Sometimes, unfortunately, our smug Wall Street Wizard also lets drop such juicy items as, "I really made a bundle on Consolidated Key Ring and Water Meter Manufacturing. Everybody else thought it was going down."

He wouldn't miss those lively radio stock market reports for the world:

"Talon Slide Fastener opened at a new low, gradually worked upward and closed at its peak . . . Scott Tissue hit a new bottom . . . Polaroid will be along in ten seconds . . . American Casket was down six . . . Admiral went down along with the shipbuilders . . . AT&T was busy and added an extension to yesterday's price . . . Macy's was up but wasn't telling how much . . . Carnation's early rise evaporated this afternoon . . . Checker Motors jumped one, two, three, four . . . CBS faded early in the day . . . J.C. Penney was up a nickel; International Nickel down a penny . . . Woolworth lost a dollar but caught the shoplifter . . . Sealey Mattress sagged at the close . . . Ward Baking rose . . . and rose . . . U.S. Shoe was pinched by adverse developments . . . Aetna Insurance—I can't make that out . . ."

Human nature being what it is, our part-time wolf of Wall Street doesn't feel worth mentioning the fact that the other seven stocks he holds are still way below the price he paid for them five years ago and that one of them is down to around 15% of its original cost. And he has forgotten about the few dogs he collected about ten years ago on which he dropped enough for a trip to Europe.

On Wall Street, forgetting is an art. We are told in glowing ads how a thousand dollars invested in such and such a stock forty years ago would be worth $100,000 today. We are not told that a thousand dollars invested in Stock B, or C, or D forty years ago would be worth exactly zero today.

It looks easy on paper to make a buck in the "Street"—but let's see how easy it is. Many years ago a famous study was made of 4,000 speculative accounts over a ten year period. Eighty percent of the accounts showed a final loss.

Another classic study was made of 500 accounts between July 1901 and March 1903. The transactions in these accounts were almost all confined to one stock—U.S. Steel. Interestingly, the price of U.S. Steel at the beginning and at the end was virtually the same. What was the result? Three hundred forty-three accounts ended up with a loss, and 52 accounts just about broke even. Seventeen others were indefinite, although each purchaser took up his stock at a hefty loss. Only 88 accounts showed a profit at the end. Imagine, if you will, what the result would have been had the price of U.S. Steel closed sharply lower at the end of the period.

Still, the man in the street believes he can outwit the market. It seldom occurs to him that he is matching wits with the best financial brains in the country, and that every time he buys a share of stock, he buys it from someone who is selling it and who believes the price is going DOWN.

On paper, it looks easy, as we've said. A stock is selling at 7. The small investor reasons that he'll buy 50 shares, sell them at 8 and make himself a quick $50. Too often he forgets—or neglects to learn—that because he is buying fewer than 100 shares, he must pay 1/8 of a dollar premium. On top of that, there's the commission, which now runs about $13. So his cost price is not 7, but more nearly 7 3/8.

The months go by and our investor friend has a very common experience (it's truly amazing how common it is): the stock doesn't go up, it goes down. A year later the stock finally creeps back up to 7, and our friend jumps at the opportunity to "break even." He sells.

Because he's selling an odd lot—fewer than 100 shares—he must again pay the 1/8 of a point premium, plus commission, plus taxes. When he receives his confirmation slip from his broker, he is stunned. It shows that he has only about $330 coming to him. Instead of breaking even, he has lost about 10% of his money—15% if you consider the interest he would have received had he put his money in a bank instead.

"When the average man buys 100 shares of United States Steel at 60 and sees it drop to 56 he isn't especially concerned," wrote Burton Crane in *The Sophisticated Investor*. "After all, that's what usually happens to his investments."

And this, from another highly respected investment authority, Rudolph L. Weissman: " . . . my own conviction (is) that attempts to beat the market are utterly pernicious for anyone but the skilled, experienced trader . . . "

And in his book, *How to Gain Security and Financial Independence*, Ira U. Cobleigh says: "Frequently there are stockholders who seem to think they can go in and buy stocks at a low price and sell them at a high price, and by trading in and out of the market can glean a fortune for themselves. Not one person in a hundred is successful in such a method, although the opportunities in the market seem so attractive that many thousands of misguided investors every year attempt this in-and-out, or butter-churn, type of trading.

"If some of the smartest men in Wall Street, men with the best connections and with plenty of financial resources, cannot make money trading in and out of the market, where do you expect to come off with such a policy?"

All right, then, if short-term trading is the royal road to ruin, how about buying good stocks for the long haul? Haven't sizable fortunes been built up by just such a policy? Yes, and sizable losses too, no matter how blue the chips.

The Myth of Wall Street is also part of the Myth of "People's Capitalism." Heartwarming advertisements tell us that stock is held by big people and little people all over the country, but they do not tell us that a few big people own almost all the stock. A Ford Foundation report entitled "Characteristics of Stock Ownership," released in September 1963, revealed that only 0.1 percent of the taxpaying population owned nearly 20 percent of all the stock in this country! Furthermore, it was brought out, the relatively small group of Americans whose incomes are above $25,000 own almost half of all the stock!

As an example, J. Paul Getty, president of Getty Oil Company, alone controlled 12,570,939 shares of that company, worth more than $300 million. For purposes of comparison, this one holding was worth more than the combined holdings of all the little investors all over the country in all stocks in all the Stock Exchange's Monthly Investment Plans!

Richard King Mellon of Pittsburgh still owned 4,003,502

shares of Gulf Oil Corporation stock, worth $200 million, after selling off 750,000 shares. Reportedly, he also owned 602,534 shares of Mellon National Bank and Trust Co. ($51 million), 1,152,752 shares of Aluminum Company of America ($71 million), and 240,000 shares of General Motors Corporation ($18 million plus).

Now that's a portfolio!

And Richard wasn't the only holder of Gulf stock in the family. Paul Mellon owned 2,843,852 shares ($141 million), and his sister Sarah owned 4,785,731 ($237 million).

Then there's Henry B. du Pont, one of whose holdings was 360,527 shares of Christiana Securities, worth $80 million; Henry Ford II, $80 million in Ford stock; Benson Ford, $95 million in Ford stock; William C. Ford, $99 million in Ford stock; William L. McNight, 2,738,082 shares of Minnesota Mining and Manufacturing worth $167 million; Archibald G. Bush, 1,697,385 shares same stock, worth $103 million; W.M. Keck, 101,946 shares of Superior Oil (nearly a quarter of all the shares outstanding), worth $140 million.

Pointed out the *New York Times:* "All of these holders wield a great influence in corporate board rooms. In practically every instance, the rich differ from the average shareowner because they almost always can be assured a representation on the board of directors.

"Because of this, they know more fully what is going on. . . ."

And we haven't mentioned investment companies, pension funds, and the other institutional investors that have now squeezed out individual investors in terms of volume on the stock exchanges.

Then what are *your* chances of winning in Wall Street?

Sixty-two percent of the vending machines in the New York subways do not work. Despite this, thousands of riders daily feed them coins—and most of them lose their money. In the stock market, the odds against your winning are not so easy to come by. Most of the surveys seem to have been taken so long ago that they bear little relevance to modern conditions, and it is difficult to avoid the suspicion that they were discontinued because of what they revealed: most investors lose.

Richard Ney, outspoken investment advisor, gadfly of the financial establishment, and author of the bestseller, *The Wall Street Jungle,* says that 99% "come out with the dirty end of the stick."

The figure may not be exact—but if it is anywhere in the ball park, 30 million investors have about as much chance of winning in the stock market as New York's straphangers have of scoring with the vending machines.

Nevertheless, some investors *do* win. Therefore, it is *possible* to win.

Some investors win by buying Polaroid, others lose by buying Polaroid. Some win by buying IBM, others lose by buying IBM. Some win by buying AT&T, others lose by buying AT&T, etc. Few ever realize the simple truths from this abundant evidence. Instead, they continue to subscribe to investment services, seek out tips, play hunches, buy financial magazines, and waste their lives and fortunes on a futile search for the answer to the riddle. Perhaps they bought National Student Marketing for $36 a share in December of 1969 and saw it plop to a buck a share five months later. Or bought Performance Systems at $23—in November 1972, not worth the price of a subway token. Or Four Seasons Nursing, worth $91 a share in October of 1969 and now bankrupt.

What simple truths could have saved all these people?

There are two. The first is: It isn't what you buy—it's how you buy it!

The second simple truth was expressed most recently by "Brutus," author of *Confessions of a Stockbroker:* "You've got to be a loser on a short-term basis in the market."

David Babson, a pioneer in the investment counseling business and one of the most highly respected forecasters of stock market trends, was a lonely voice in the 1960's crying out against "a speculative orgy and a national crap game." One of his famous quotes deserves repeating here: "There may be nothing very exciting about buying for the long pull—but it works."

Appearing on TV's "Wall Street Week," he was asked to give an investment philosophy. His answer: "I think that investors ought to own the very best and most successful companies they can and keep them. I don't think they ought to be looking for market turns and try to sell them . . . The big difference (today) is that you have to pay these high multiples for the most attractive growth companies, but there comes a period every once in awhile when you can buy them at a significant drop in their multiples—like May 1970."

Moderator: "David, in the 1960's your Mutual Fund took seven years to double and some Funds were doubling in months. Since then your Fund has held up while some of those Go-Go Funds went-went. Now I just want to ask you to tell us the truth. Wasn't there any point along the way when you began to wonder whether you ought to change your philosophy?"

"No. No, not when you could see the balloon being inflated, being blown up, you didn't have to be an investment genius to know that it was going to break someday."

And finally, this off-the-cuff advice to novice investors delivered on the same program on another occasion by G.M. Loeb, the dean of Wall Street. "Go slow, and take your time and not expect too much; and particularly do not think that all the profits are in exotic things. Some very commonplace things, if you look at the difference between the highs and lows in the course of the year, will give you a very good return."

That is the philosophy behind *Superpower Investing.*

The Men Who Make Sure You Don't Walk Away Winners

2

Investing your money may be likened unto climbing a ladder with each succeeding rung 5% weaker than the last. To play the game you take a bag containing as many gold pieces as you dare and mount the first step. A window opens at that level and a beaming face appears that very much resembles that of your friendly banker. He deposits in your bag 5% more gold pieces and shuts the window in your face. You have a heavier burden now than when you started, but the first rung of the ladder is extremely sturdy and offers little risk. If you mount the next step, a window will open and a slightly less friendly gent will drop 5% more gold coins into your bag. He is slightly less friendly because his office is on the second floor and he has to lug a bag of gold up a flight of stairs to work every day.

You now have a burden that is 10% heavier than when you

started, but the second rung of the ladder, though 5% weaker than the first, seems substantial enough to support the additional weight. Besides, if it *should* break, you'd fall only a short distance and probably not even lose your balance when you hit the ground. For that matter, you speculate, even if you fell from the *third* rung, you probably wouldn't even sprain an ankle. Particularly if you were *expecting* to fall.

At the fourth step the window opens and a sly face appears. "What do you want?" Sly Face says.

Startled, you retort, "What do you mean, what do I want? I want my 5%."

"Sorry about that. I thought maybe you—never mind. Maybe coming down. Here's your 5%."

What a strange fellow! What did he *think* you wanted?

The next rung creaks a little, but your fears are dispelled by the warm, kindly face of the old gent in the window. "Kinda high, aren't you, young fella?"

"I don't think so," you respond. "Aside from a little creaking, the rung seems safe enough."

The old man frowns. "That rung may seem safe enough now, but what will it do when I put 5% more gold in your bag?"

"I didn't start out with a heavy load to begin with," you answer, "so I don't think 5% more at this point will make that much difference."

"Well," he says, "at least I'll give you credit for that much intelligence. But let me tell you something, young fella. I been around a long time, and I seen a lot of young fellas like you.

There was a young fella like you back in ought five or ought six or thereabouts, I recollect, and *he* thought that rung was safe enough. It was, too, till I up and put the 5% in his bag."

Your hands suddenly feel slippery. "What happened?" you croak.

"Dangdest thing I ever saw. I cautioned him, you know, much as I'm cautioning you here now, but he didn't pay no mind, not him! Took the 5%, you know, and the rung held him, all right, but the next rung up didn't."

"You mean the next rung up broke when he got another 5% up there?"

"Mean no such thing! Mean the rung gave way before he had a chance to collect!"

"I'm sorry to hear that," you say, "but if it's all the same to you I'll take the risk."

"Looks like a storm comin' up, young fella. If the storm catches you high up the ladder, you're done for. Seen it myself in ought nine. Or was it 29? No matter."

"I'll take my chances," you say, and the old man hurls 5% more gold into your bag. "You just wait, smart aleck hippie!" he shouts, but you've already moved up a rung and found that it would hold you. The window opens and a younger man appears. "What was all the racket about?" he says.

"It was that old man down there," you explain. "He didn't want me to come any higher."

The man in the window laughs. "Oh, that! Charley's a nice guy but old fashioned as hell."

You laugh in relief. "Then you think I should go higher?"

The merriment disappears from the man's face. "I didn't say that. Don't even suggest that I said that. If you tell the Ladder Commission I said that, I'll deny the whole thing."

"Then you think I should go back down?"

"I didn't say that."

"But if I don't go up and I don't go down, how the hell do I get off this ladder?"

He smiles a twisted, silver-glittering smile. "Give me half your profit and I'll let you in the window. Then you can walk down the stairs."

"Half my profit! That's ridiculous! What kind of game are you running?"

"How do you think we make a living?"

"I'd have to be a fool to go along with that. Why, if I wanted to play it safe I'd just collect my 5% and go back down the ladder."

"Take a look at that rung you're standing on."

"It looks all right to me."

"That's because you don't know anything about ladders. But this is my *business.* Ever hear of the 18th Law of Thermodynamics? Velocity torque ratios? I guarantee you that if I give you 5% that rung is going to collapse like a wet Kleenex."

"You're just trying to scare me. If I were that timid I'd tell you to keep your 5% and I'd go back down that ladder with the profit I already have."

Now the man laughs. "Ah, innocence! Let's assume I *do* give you 5% and the rung doesn't break. Let's assume then that you decide not to go higher but to go back down the ladder. You will be 5% heavier, my friend."

"True, but the next rung down is 5% stronger than this one."

"Really? If you knew anything about mass times parallel support ratios, you'd know that when you descend a ladder you place 6% more weight on the rungs than when you ascend a ladder. So even if you decline my 5% and try to go back down, you are going to hit that next rung with 6% more weight. Which means one percent more risk than when you first stepped on it. Kersplatt!"

"In any event, I think I'll go up. I knew a guy who went way up and he said he made a lot of money."

"Don't believe everything you hear. People tend to exaggerate in the ladder business, especially extension ladders which aren't really as long as they say because of the overlap requirement."

"Just give me my 5%!"

"Okay, here you are. Hmm, I'm really surprised that rung is still holding. But you're really in for it now!"

"What do you mean?"

"Even if you decide to go down now, you will hit the rung below with 6% more risk than when you first stepped on it. See, here it is right here on the chart. Better give me two-thirds of your profit and come inside."

"Two-thirds! A minute ago you said half!"

"That was then. You're heavier now and your risk is greater."

Up you climb, ignoring the warnings until, sweating and struggling, you finally manage to lug your heavy bag of gold to the 20th rung. The window opens.

"BOO!" shouts the little man. "Scared you, didn't I?"

"You darn near made me fall!" you cry angrily.

"Six of one, half a dozen of the other," he chortles. "You're going to fall anyway. If I give you 5%, your burden will be 100% heavier than when you started. And you know, don't you, that this rung is nearly 100% weaker than the first one. You poor boob, you're about 200 times more likely to fall from here than from the first rung. What's more, I heard a rumor that the sidepieces of this ladder are defective. The whole shebang could come apart any minute now. The company that made it is under Congressional investigation."

"You're . . . really vicious!"

"How do you think I got this high? Now, tell you what I'm gonna do . . ."

"Hurry! Can't hang on much longer . . ."

"For only 75% of your profit I am going to let you come through my window to safety. Listen, it's better than losing everything, isn't it?"

"Yes, *yes,* for God's sake let me in!"

He helps you inside and you lie trembling on the floor while he counts your gold. Finally you get up. The little man watches you warily. "Before you do anything foolish," he says, "remember that you can get five years for hitting a man with glasses." He flashes a golden grin. "However, for only 25% more of your profits, I will tell you a secret that will help you climb this ladder safely in the future. Deal?"

"Deal," you gasp. "What's . . . the secret?"

The little man chuckles. " 'Experience keeps a dear school, but fools will learn in no other.' "

* * *

In the world of investment—as in every other world—you have to give up something to get something. There are no free lunches, and every presumed advantage is, in fact, a trade-off. When you buy a sports car, you sacrifice safety and comfort for speed. When you buy a motorized gadget to perform some job you had been doing manually, it costs you money, risk of injury, and frustration and expense when it breaks down. Want a bigger house? Fine, but be prepared to pay more to buy it, heat it, cool it, furnish it, maintain it, and keep up the taxes. Want to move to the suburbs to escape crime? Many have—and have found to their regret that the cost in lack of services, wasted commutation hours, soaring taxes, reduced family life, and countless other suburban living disadvantages just about cancel out the benefits.

Want safety for your money? Buy a U.S. Savings Bond or put your money in a Federally insured bank or Savings and Loan.

Need a little more than five or six percent? You'll have to increase your risk a little, perhaps by buying corporate bonds or preferred stock—or, if you can't afford the risk, do a little extra paperwork to increase your bank interest, as will be seen later.

Need some growth for your money? Again, you'll have to

expose your capital to greater risk, perhaps by buying common stock in blue chip companies. Your income may be smaller and less dependable, but there is a possibility that your investment will increase in value over the years.

Need high voltage growth for your capital? Here you may buy shares of smaller or more speculative companies offering a greater potential for profit—and for loss.

Over the years, many theories have evolved in an attempt to make investing more of a science than a gamble. One of the most popular plans for reducing the risk of buying stock is called Dollar Cost Averaging. Eliminating the frustration of trying to decide *when* to buy, it involves purchasing stock on a regular basis with the same amount of money. If the stock declines, your money will buy more shares. If the stock advances, your money will buy fewer shares. Though the plan works best if the stock goes into a long decline following your first purchase and then recovers, you will almost always make out better with Dollar Cost Averaging than you would buying impulsively and erratically for the simple reason that because your fixed dollar buys more shares at lower prices and fewer shares at higher prices, your average cost per share tends to be lower.

In the accompanying Dollar Cost Averaging chart, the investor bought $100 worth of stock every month. When he made his first purchase, the stock was selling at $10 a share; and his $100 bought him 10 shares. The following month, because the stock had declined in price to $9, the investor's $100 bought him 11.11 shares. Subsequent declines in price enabled the investor's $100 to purchase larger numbers of shares until, at the bottom of the market, his $100 bought him 20 shares—twice as many as his first $100 had bought!

Thus, while the stock had declined in price 50%, the systematic investor had acquired more than 84 shares at an average cost of only $7.09 per share! At this point he has lost 30% of his money, but he would have lost *half* if he'd invested his entire $600 in one lump sum.

Now it gets interesting. If the stock goes back to its original price of $10, the investor will realize a profit of some 41%. And if the price advances to $14.19 a share, the investor will have doubled his money! Commission costs and dividends have not been considered as these tend to approximate and cancel out each other.

Though Dollar Cost Averaging has been described as the nearest thing to foolproof investing, there are two important conditions that must be met to insure its success. First is the selection of a stock that will eventually go up in price. It is not necessarily true that a blue chip stock will go up. In a recent ten-year period, such high quality Dow Jones industrial stocks as U.S. Steel, International Paper, Allied Chemical, and Aluminum Co. ended up lower than when they started, and many others eked out such insignificant gains that anyone who bought them in a Dollar Cost Averaging program probably incurred a loss along with many of those who bought them sporadically along the way.

The second condition is fidelity to your original plan. When your stock drops, will you continue to make your purchases on schedule—or will you begin to have doubts about the whole thing; worry about throwing "good money after bad"? Equally, will you have the *money* to continue the plan? *It is incalculably better to set your sights a little lower with investments smaller than you can afford—and continue to invest through thick and thin—than to step off boldly with a grandiose plan you will drop at the first sign of trouble in Wall Street or in your own personal finances.*

Dollar Cost Averaging involves buying the same dollar amount of stock at fixed intervals. The example given here assumes a steady decline in the price per share. As everyone knows, it doesn't often happen that way. There are peaks and valleys on the way down as well as on the way up. In each valley your dollar will buy more shares, and on each peak fewer. The results of *your* Dollar Cost Averaging program may be more or less inspiring than the example given. For instance, during a decline, the price might hover near $8 a share for three months before dropping further, forcing you to buy three batches at that price. That would increase your average cost per share and lessen your eventual profits. On the other hand, the price might plummet from 9 to 7 before your next purchase date rolls around, and instead of getting only 12½ shares for your money, you'd get more than 14.

By removing much of the guesswork and risk, dollar cost averaging has proved to be a most valuable approach to successful long-term investing.

DOLLAR COST AVERAGING

Price Per Share	Number Of Shares Purchased	Cost	Number Of Shares Now Owned	Total Investment To Date
$10	10.00	$100	10.00	$100
$ 9	11.11	$100	21.11	$200
$ 8	12.50	$100	33.61	$300
$ 7	14.29	$100	47.90	$400
$ 6	16.67	$100	64.57	$500
$ 5	20.00	$100	84.57	$600

Dollar Cost Averaging —A Golden Trap for the Pennies of Fools 3

I have a friend who is a fairly typical investor. In other words, none too bright. Yet he's read all the books, knows all the jargon of the Street, and loves to rap about investment philosophy. Maybe you've seen him some lunch hour at your nearby Merrill Lynch, or Neuberger Loeb, or Hardy & Co., his breath faintly redolent of pastrami, his stomach gurgling with fermenting martinis, cheesecake, and coffee. He consistently loses money in the market, and consistently takes his maximum tax loss every year (so it shouldn't be a total loss); but he is confident that soon the tide will be reversed. Once he nearly had hysterics over a newspaper cartoon showing a bum on a park bench reading the *Wall Street Journal.* The bum was saying something like, "Oh, so *that's* it—*buy* low and *sell* high!"

The year 1970 was a turning point. It was a year that my

friend—and many others like him—finally woke up. I happen to have access to his records going all the way back to 1961, and it's a sad, sad story. I want you to hear it for yourself. The microphone is hidden inside the tobacco jar of my pipe rack, but most of the tape is intelligible, if not intelligent.

"Let's see, my first loss was in January—a Brunswick Call Option that I bought in October of '61 for $256.36. It became worthless in January, so it's a total loss. That sure was surprising. The bowling boom was on and Brunswick was going through the roof. I forget if it was *Forbes* or *Barron's* or one of the others, but the only question at the time was whether Brunswick or American Machine and Foundry was going to end up with the lion's share. I guess nobody did. Who would have thought back then that the whole thing was going to burst like a bubble? Anyway, I thought I'd play it smart and buy a Call Option on a hundred shares. That way I could make a big profit on a small investment. I even thought the ad in the *Times* was a misprint. I couldn't believe you could buy an Option on Brunswick for only a couple of hundred dollars when the stock was selling in the sixties. But when I called the Option dealer he said no, it was no misprint, and so I bought it. And then Brunswick took a nose dive."

"I see that only a few days before your Option expired, you bought 10 shares of Brunswick for $420.36, and sold them a week later for $387.98, for a loss of $32.38. If Brunswick had dropped all the way down to the 40's why did you go out and buy 10 shares?"

"Because I knew by that time I'd already lost on the Option, and I figured Brunswick would soon turn around and go back up, so I wanted to make my money back."

"But why did you sell a week later if you felt like that?"

"Because Brunswick kept dropping and I wanted to cut my

losses. In the old days I would have held on and lost even more, but then I read this book that tells you to cut losses, so I did—which was lucky, because the stock went down to 8 or something and never did come back."

"A few days later you bought 30 Hazel Bishop, and then 20 shares more in February, for a total of $588.03. You sold all 50 in March for a profit of $30.15. Well, at least you made a profit."

"Oh, yeah, but I never could figure that stock. I traded in it earlier. For awhile there I thought it was going to be another Revlon. That's what they were saying and all, and at one time they were sponsoring one of those big quiz shows just like Revlon, but nothing ever happened. That was when it was called Lanolin Plus. I guess I was lucky to get out of it that time with a profit. Once I was so sure the stock was going to move I bought 300 shares at 7 or so and was using body English on it."

"Body English?"

"Yes, I was going out and buying their products. They had all kinds of products. You see, they didn't have all that many shares outstanding, so I figured every dollar profit the company made would help, because if the stock is selling at ten times earnings or so, every penny per share profit would cause the stock to go up ten cents. I had this idea that, hell, if I bought a hundred dollars or so worth of their products, that I might single-handedly cause the stock to go up some. And also, by buying the merchandise at the same drugstore, their supply would soon be depleted and they would have to order more. I would also 'talk it up,' you know, comment to the clerk how good the products were, hoping maybe she would buy some too and tell her friends; even steal some for that matter. See, I had 300 shares, and if it went up a dollar I'd have made $300."

"Anyway, in February of 1961 you bought 172 shares of Rowe Price New Horizons Fund for $1,998.64 and dumped them in November of 1962 for $1,517.04, a loss of $481.60. A Mutual Fund is a long-term investment. Why did you sell?"

"You know how it was in '62. Everybody was selling out. I panicked, I guess. If it had been a regular type Fund I might have held on, I don't know, but it *was* kind of speculative, and I figured this was the wrong time to be in a speculative Fund. It sure dropped."

"It sure came back, though, didn't it?"

"I get sick every time I see it."

"I notice a slight move here away from individual securities into Mutual Funds."

"I gave up, that's why. I figured if I can't make it on my own, maybe they can make it for me. Besides, it was taking up too much of my time. I spent three or four hours every night reading up on finance. If it weren't for that, I'd probably have lost everything."

"Yes, but you're buying and selling Funds the same way you did individual securities. Here, in May of 1962, you redeemed 91 shares of Energy Fund which you had accumulated variously . . . $201.87 invested in March of 1960, and thereafter it looks like . . . hundred, hundred, hundred . . . it looks like a hundred dollars a month up until October of 1961. A couple months you missed, maybe, and maybe a couple months you sent two checks, but all in all it seems to me that you had a fairly good Dollar Cost Averaging program going."

"Yeah, I'd read somewhere that this would average you out and that you would almost certainly come out ahead over a period of time."

"You came out ahead $40. Not very much for a total investment of some $2,000. You could have made more than that in a bank—and saved a lot of time and effort. I suppose you sold this Fund for the same reason in 1962—fear?"

"Everybody was afraid. I figured the market was going no place but down."

"Yes, but why did you stop your Dollar Cost Averaging program in October of 1961 instead of keeping it up? There wasn't much fear around then."

"I don't know. I guess maybe I figured I could do better on my own . . . ."

"And even in May of 1962, when you cashed it in, the price hadn't quite gone down below your original purchase."

"I was afraid it was going to, though—and it did. It's high now, though . . . which is typical."

"Well, at least you didn't lose money on it. But you did too many things wrong. You skipped a couple of months, you sent two checks instead of one a couple of months, you stopped your program too soon, and you sold in a bear market. And yet, despite all this, you still managed to avoid a loss, which ought to demonstrate to you the value of Dollar Cost Averaging.

"I guess, but really I've had it with Dollar Cost. I own a Fund that's selling now in 1972 for less than it was six or seven years ago. It was a long climb up over the years, and I was buying lots and lots of stock at eight, nine, and ten dollars a share. Now it's down to six. If you think I'm going to keep buying that dog when I've lost half of my money, you're mistaken."

"I guess that's a weakness of Dollar Cost Averaging. Too many people behave the way you do. They either lose interest on the way up because they think they can do better with hit or miss investing, or they panic at the bottom; become discouraged. It's human nature."

"Thanks. I'm glad you admit it. Dollar Cost Averaging! Can't you fellas come up with anything better than *that?*"

The $153,900,000 Chase Manhattan Bank Mutual Fund Caper 4

In February of 1970, the "biggest and most dangerous contest ever let loose in the investment world" began in New York City. The Chase Manhattan Bank, in an attempt to locate the finest financial brains in the nation, gave each of its contestants—the 36 leading stock brokerage firms in the nation—$100 million as an imaginary stake to see which man could do the most with it in the stock market. With access to virtually unlimited analysis and research assistance within their firms, the contestants embarked upon the construction of their paper portfolio with gusto. Most of them had about 13 well-paid investment analysts at their disposal. One, the man from Merrill Lynch, had 80. Contestants were instructed to phone their imaginary buy and sell orders to one of Chase's four referees and explain the reason behind the action. The Great Money Game was more than a game for the Chase Bank; with some $13 billion in trust and pension funds to manage, they were more than a little interested in locating the investment wizards who could do the best job for them. And, since "David's Bank" is anything but cheap, they guaranteed the three top winners $180,000 a year in commissions—in *real* money!

On February 27th, the day the game began, the phone rang in the office of Ralph Cox at the Chase Bank. Cox, one of the four "referees," heard the caller say, "This is SYNCHROVEST. Buy $5 million worth of Rowe Price New Horizons Fund."

"Buy *what?*" Cox exploded with laughter, realizing he was the victim of a put-on; but the caller had hung up.

"What was that all about?" said Joe Debe, father of the Paper Portfolio Program idea.

"Some nut," Cox laughed. "Called himself SYNCHROVEST. He must have heard about our money game. He wants us to—get this: he gave us a buy order for $5 million worth of some Mutual Fund! New Horizons, I think."

"Did I hear correctly?" said Erwin Zeuschner, another portfolio referee. "I hope it isn't one of our contestants who made that call."

"You never know," said James M. Lane, executive vice president. "Maybe he ran out of ideas."

"It has got to be a nut," laughed Cox. "New Horizons is a no-load and no broker is going to recommend that and miss an 8½% commission, even if it's only on paper."

On the last business day of every month, the mysterious caller telephoned his buy order to Chase Manhattan. His stock selection was always the same—Rowe Price New Horizons Fund; only the amount of his purchase varied.

Finally, on December 31, 1970, the mystery man, who by now had become a running gag around the Chase plant, called for the last time: "Buy $1,484,878 worth of Rowe Price New Horizons Fund," he said in a muffled voice. "That completes my $100 million investment."

"But the game isn't over yet," Cox laughed. "We have several more months to go."

"It's over for me," said the caller. "I'm leaving for an extended vacation in the Bahamas. See you."

The Paper Portfolio Program stumbled along. Half of the players performed so disappointingly that they were quietly advised to "take a rest for awhile." Some bombed so badly that whenever they called Chase with a buy or sell order, a secretary advised them that none of the referees was in. Their names were struck from the roster and replaced by eager would-be contestants on the waiting list.

"Well, that does it," said Joe Debe on October 31, 1971. "The top winner ran the $100 million to about $150 million—50%. Not bad. Not bad at all."

"Hey," said Lane, "just for the heck of it, how did that nut do—that SYNCHROVEST guy who used to call up to buy—what was it—New Horizons Fund?"

Cox chuckled and looked at his records. "It's selling for about $31. It was about $27 when he started buying, so all he made was a lousy four points or so. I know a hundred Funds that did better than that." He swiveled around in his chair and punched a button on the computer. "It's costing us $100,000 a year to run this baby. Might as well get some use of it. Let's see exactly how our mystery caller did—just for the fun of it."

SYNCHROVEST

Date	Price	Investment	Shares Bought	Shares Owned	Total Investment	Cost Per Share	Credit Balance
2/70	26.74	$5,000,000	186,986	186,986	$5,000,000	26.74	$95,000,000
3/70	25.53	$9,000,000	352,526	539,512	$14,000,000	25.95	$86,000,000
4/70	20.78	$26,840,000	1,291,627	1,831,139	$40,840,000	22.30	$59,160,000
5/70	19.00	$15,265,600	803,453	2,634,592	$56,105,600	21.30	$43,894,400
6/70	18.31	$13,312,048	727,037	3,361,629	$69,417,648	20.65	$30,582,352
7/70	19.47	$8,914,059	457,836	3,819,465	$78,331,707	20.51	$21,668,293
8/70	20.34	$6,333,415	311,377	4,130,842	$84,665,122	20.50	$15,334,878
9/70	22.54	$4,550,000	201,863	4,332,705	$89,215,122	20.59	$10,784,878
10/70	22.03	$4,750,000	215,615	4,548,320	$93,965,122	20.66	$6,034,878
11/70	22.83	$4,550,000	199,299	4,747,619	$98,515,122	20.75	$1,484,878
12/70	24.36	$1,484,878	60,956	4,808,575	$100,000,000		0
Dist. 1/71	(25.96)	$2,981,317	114,843	4,923,418		20.31	

PRICE 10/71 AT CONCLUSION OF "PP" PROGRAM: $31.26
TOTAL VALUE OF SHARES: $153,906,047.00 (53.9%)

"Good Lord," said Lane. "And he stopped investing last year! He beat everybody! And look at September! Three months off the bottom of the market and he had a *profit!* What were his results, say, a month ago?"

Cox punched the button.

59.4% said the computer.

"Oh my," said Debe. "How about two months ago?"

Cox punched the button.

53.8% said the computer.

"How about four months from now?" said the janitor.

"What are you—a nut?" said Lane. "How can the computer tell what the price of the stock will be four months from now?"

"Well," said the janitor, "you called *him* a nut, too!"

Cox punched the button.

100% said the computer, and added: GOOD NIGHT, DAVID.

Except for the facts about the Chase Manhattan Bank's Paper Portfolio Program and the results obtained, the foregoing scenario was entirely fictitious. SYNCHROVEST did not exist then.

But it exists now.

SYNCHROVEST —The Miracle of Superpower Investing 5

What to Buy, When to Buy, and When to Sell are the holy trinity of Wall Street, and outside the church a multitude of vendors sell indulgences. Indeed, their numbers seem almost as great as the worshippers within. This Jeremiah sees nothing but gloom, and for only 30 shekels (tax deductible) he will spell it out for you so graphically you will roll in the ashes and call for the mountains to fall on top of you. Dum Spiro Spero over there sees nothing but sunshine, and for 30 zlotys will tell you why in such glowing terms you'll spend your envelope full of Kennedy halves to get your share of it. And all around are high priests hawking charts, computer tapes, price/earnings' ratios, turnaround situations, industry trends, and various other mystic paraphernalia guaranteeing you salvation.

Over there, that old bearded prophet with the scepter who is haranguing the crowd—his job is to lend dignity to the scene, to sanctify it, to endow it with high purpose. They call him the Old Prophet of the Church Steps.

"I believe!" cries an old lady. "I have Kentucky Fried Chicken!"

An oldster in the crowd shouts, "What about 1929?"

The prophet's eyes flash fire. "Call no man free who fears his father's gods!"

A hippie pushes forward. "What about pollution?"

"A great growth industry!" answers the prophet. "I see acres of factories producing pollution control equipment . . ."

"How many who have come here have actually been saved?" shouts a stringy-haired girl in glasses. "One thousand dollars invested in AT&T 43 years ago is worth only $819 today! And because of the depreciation of the dollar, that $819 is actually worth only $270!"

"Faith! You must have faith!" cries the prophet. "And patience! You young kids today are too impatient!"

A large part of America's 30 million shareholders spend much of their time and money at these pre-service gatherings. And, despite the fact that salvation is not forthcoming for most of them, they return again and again hoping for the miracle. Surely, they think, if so many others worship here, this must be the true church. Perhaps my faith is not strong enough . . . .

We will not attend. The market will go up, or the market will go down. It is of no concern to us because "Now is the accepted time; behold, now is the day of salvation." *All that we want from the market is already there, at this time.* Whether it rise or fall, it will build our perfect pyramid.

We shall not attempt to guess the direction of the market, not burden ourselves with needless grief that we have either missed out on the boom or have placed our funds in jeopardy.

The design flaw in the Dollar Cost Averaging pyramid is that its base is not wide enough, and after a prolonged period of rising prices we may find our tall narrow structure vulnerable to a storm. But how do we make the base larger, the pyramid more symmetrical?

We must attempt to develop an alternative method to Dollar Cost Averaging, for while Dollar Cost has been praised on the one hand for improving the performance of the average investor, it has been damned on the other for producing only average results at best, and exposing the investor to stunning losses at worst. Dollar Cost cannot meaningfully improve our investment results because it fails to adjust for the historical time difference between bull and bear markets. Protracted periods of high prices result in a top-heavy portfolio—too many shares purchased at high prices. Investing the same amount of money monthly, the investor is not given the time during brief bear markets to reduce his average cost per share significantly—as many Dollar Cost Averagers have learned to their dismay.

Richard Ney, in his eye-opening book, *The Wall Street Jungle*, gives us as one of his rules in buying stock, "Restrict purchases to stocks that have declined at least 35 to 50 percent from their highs," pointing out that such a tactic can cover a multitude of blunders. It is a point well made.

Another famous exponent of this principle was the noted investment counselor and business forecaster, Roger W. Babson. In 1903 he and his wife started a Fund with $1200. Fifteen years later, they added $100,000. That was the sum total of their investment. Although they put no more into the Fund, they made substantial withdrawals from it along the way—sizable gifts to educational institutions, dividend withdrawals for living expenses, etc.—and yet on December 31, 1953, the Fund was worth more than $5,000,000! The method? "Buy good stocks when most people are *impatient* to sell them and hence the stocks are too cheap; this requires courage. Have *patience* to hold these stocks until most people are impatient to buy stocks, hence stocks are too high; then sell. This also requires courage . . . . Proper timing, courage and patience are the basis of 80 percent of today's fortunes." (Italics Babson's)

Babson emphasized the importance of having cash, and the value of diversification. "The theory of having a *portion* of one's money invested in a selective group of stocks is sound, providing the price paid is sound . . . ." (Italics Babson's)

Babson's investment philosophy reflected techniques of the British financial titans at the turn of the century. By keeping their overhead down and cutting expenses to the bone, these bankers could afford to *wait*. They would enter the market only once every half dozen years or so to buy stocks at their lows and sell them a few years later when the inevitable boom arrived. Then they would sit back and chuckle through the inevitable crash and panic. With this method they accumulated vast fortunes and built the world-famous estates throughout England, many of which now stand deserted, monuments to the folly of their descendants who, scorning their "square" ancestors, turned impatiently to speculation with ruinous results.

Let us be about our father's business. Let us build our castles.

I give you SYNCHROVEST—nicknamed FLAB-SLAB by our engineers ("Float Like a Butterfly. Sting Like a Bee"). One engineer claims that he incorporated the recursive function theory and quantum mechanics in it. Another insists that it utilizes the regenerative braking principle with just a hint of rational energy accounting, a pinch of Pythagorean geometry, and a smidgen of patterned transformations to taste; withal a living, breathing thing, constantly digesting relationships between numbers and acting in the best interests of its operator. As chief of the top secret crash program to build SYNCHROVEST, it cost me three solid years at the drawing board, a gross of pencils, reams of paper, and a tub of Preparation H.

SYNCHROVEST trails every price change; there is no escape. When the market lures it upward toward disaster, the FLAB-SLAB butterfly playfully tags along, alights daintily on the gaudy prices, flits hither and yon as it samples the exotic nectar at these delirious elevations; but when the market falls, FLAB-SLAB metamorphoses into an angry hornet after blood, stinging the daylights out of retreating prices, kills them dead and drags great numbers of them back to its nest.

Thus, throughout bull markets, SYNCHROVEST commits less capital than Dollar Cost Averaging; in bear markets, more. Because of this flexibility, its total dollar commitment to the market tends to trail Dollar Cost's; the balance must be placed immediately and irrevocably in a savings account to await The Call.

In examples given at the end of this chapter, SYNCHROVEST tippy-toed along with Dollar Cost Averager through the boom and down to the bottom of the market with less money invested than Dollar Cost. The results speak for themselves. SYNCHROVEST proved not only dramatically superior in preserving investment capital on the downside, but in increasing capital on the upside.

SYNCHROVEST
Operating Instructions

1. As with Dollar Cost Averaging, select an amount of

money you will be able to invest comfortably every month—an amount you are presently convinced you will be able to maintain. This is your *Planned Investment.* Multiply this figure by .75. Example: Your *Planned Investment* is $300. Multiplying that by .75 gives $225. That is your *Base Investment,* and from this day forward your *Base Investment*—not your *Planned Investment*—will be the figure you will work with. Take good care of it and keep it clean.

2. Your record sheet will look the same as it does for any accumulation program. I am adding only a *Cost Per Share* column and a *Credit Balance* column.

The *Cost Per Share* is obtained simply by dividing the total shares you own into the total amount you have invested. For the sake of simplicity, use rounded figures here and everywhere else. Thus, if you own 162.5 shares at a cost of $3,897, you divide 163 into $3,897 and come up with $24. This all-important *Cost Per Share* figure tells you at a glance what you paid for each and every share of stock you own. Obviously, if the price of your stock is now $25 a share, you have a $1 profit on each share—a total profit of $163 (163 shares x $1).

SYNCHROVEST employs the *Cost Per Share* figure as a capstan drive. Also built into the *Cost Per Share* is a clutch, a gear box, a mini-computer, and a midget investment adviser constantly examining the relationships between price and cost, always on the alert for bargains and stubbornly chary of waste. When it allows you to spend a penny, you can be sure it has a very good reason for it.

3. Every month, when your investment date rolls around, look in the paper for the *Price Per Share* of your stock. Round it off. Thus, $33.50 becomes $34, while $33.49 becomes $33.

Divide that *Price Per Share* into the last *Cost Per Share* on your record sheet. Example: Your last *Cost Per Share* was $33, while the *Price Per Share* of your stock in the newspaper is $34. Dividing $34.00 into $33.00 yields a figure of .97. *SYNCHROVEST is asking you to invest 97% of your Base Investment.* Now simply multiply your *Base Investment* by .97 and you will obtain the amount of the investment SYNCHROVEST wants you to make. Using the earlier example, if your *Base Investment* is $225, you multiply it by .97 and derive the figure 218. Write out a check for $218 and send it. And, since you *promised* in the beginning to invest $300 a month, put the balance of the money, $82, into a special savings account. Enter this figure in your final column, *Credit Balance.*

(If long division doesn't frighten you, use exact figures in all calculations. And if you own a calculator, exact results can be obtained in seconds.)

4. While your monthly investments are kinetic energy, this bank account is potential energy. *You are not to touch it unless SYNCHROVEST asks you to invest more than your Base Investment.* For example: Your current *Cost Per Share* is $34, while the *Price Per Share* of your stock in the newspaper is $33—just the opposite from the example above. You divide $33.00 into $34.00 and get 1.03. Anything above 1.00 (100) means that you must make one more calculation. First, you go ahead as usual and multiply your *Base Investment* by 1.03. If your *Base Investment* is $225, for example, multiplying that by 1.03 gives you $232. The second calculation you must make in this case is this: See that 1.03 figure? Drop the first digit, which will give you .03. *SYNCHROVEST is asking you to invest, in addition to the $232, 3% of your Credit Balance.* Multiply your *Credit Balance* by .03 to find out how much that is. Add the two figures together—the $232 and the 3% of your bank account—and you will have the correct amount to invest. Sometimes even this combined amount will be less than your *Planned Investment* ($300 in the example given earlier) and it will not even be necessary for you to dip into your bank

account. You might even have money left over. Be sure to deposit this immediately in your *Credit Balance* account. If you don't, SYNCHROVEST will make rain on your house for 30 days and 30 nights—automatically.

You will come to love every diode and varistor in SYNCHROVEST's mechanism. Possibly love will bloom when you discover that although a dollar is the difference between 9 and 10 as well as between 19 and 20, SYNCHROVEST is well aware of the percentile difference and is not at all deceived. It may happen when, to your amazement, SYNCHROVEST calls the bottom of the market with almost pinpoint accuracy and accordingly requests the highest percentage of your assets to be invested at that point. Or you may feel your heart swell with fondness for SYNCHROVEST when, for the first time in your investment history, you begin to feel *secure*, regardless of whether the market is rising or falling!

SYNCHROVEST gives the little man a break in the market for the first time. During booms especially—but even during declines!—it builds up his bank account to enable him to take advantage of cheaper prices later on. You may even doubt your sanity when, during periods of falling prices, SYNCHROVEST not only increases your investments but builds up your bank account at the same time in anticipation of still lower prices! This is no big deal, just a highly sophisticated form of integrated circuitry incorporating decision procedures, macroscopic isomorphisms, and predicate calculus.

SYNCHROVEST is absolutely immune to "share fever," the disease that is nearly always fatal to investors. It is not concerned with accumulating more shares than the Dollar Cost Averager, particularly during the first decline. Shares don't tell the story; *profit* does. SYNCHROVEST attempts to protect the investor against the savage losses often suffered by Dollar Costers and Hit or Missers, while at the same time equaling or bettering their profit. When, in the opinion of management, it becomes necessary to purchase a greater number of shares than Dollar Cost to achieve its aim, SYNCHROVEST will act. Thus, at times, SYNCHROVEST will own more shares than Dollar Cost, at other times fewer. But always it attempts to keep the investor in the profit column longer than Dollar Cost, and, following a crash, to get him well faster. Given a decline of major proportions, SYNCHROVEST could eventually present you with the kind of fortune Dollar Costers dare not even dream about.

Even critics unblinded by the hyperbolic acid that is regularly spritzed by Dollar Cost Averaging's proponents will concede that the method works well if begun at the beginning of a slump, and if the price subsequently moves into higher ground. Here, if nowhere else, Dollar Cost should shine. Yet, as we see in Chart C at the end of this chapter, Dollar Cost, despite its massive monthly investments, was unable to keep up with the smaller, intelligently-planned investments of SYNCHROVEST. Fortunately for Dollar Cost, the Fund in question performed in textbook fashion and managed a powerful finish-line kick that carried the price sharply higher and above its original. Had it not done so, Dollar Cost would *still* trail SYNCHROVEST's profit, despite its substantially larger total investment.

And even now, where is Dollar Cost? Big, clumsy, stupid, it stands bewildered with empty pockets contemplating its paltry, pitiful ephemera of a $31 victory over SYNCHROVEST, a Pyrrhic victory purchased at the shattering cost of $1,598! (It is not really a victory, of course, as SYNCHROVEST earned more than that in bank interest.)

And where is SYNCHROVEST? He has been hoarding his energy. He has not been running at full strength. His friction clutch prevented his running away with the race. But he has done his job and now, with a hefty bank account, he is prepping for the big one. A decline at this point would result in an awesome advantage for SYNCHROVEST in the number of shares it could buy.

Finally, SYNCHROVEST could be shown in a much better light. Few Funds soar 100% without looking back as Rowe Price did, piling up so much money in the bank without permitting SYNCHROVEST buying opportunities along the way; and few individual stocks fluctuate so gently as the New York Stock Exchange Composite Index of all stocks, again failing to provide many buying opportunities. It is obvious, too, that since bank interest has not been added to the *Credit Balance* in the charts to follow (interest amounting to hundreds of dollars), the final results would have proved far more striking; *for not only does bank interest provide SYNCHROVEST with extra profits, it permits SYNCHROVEST to purchase more shares when its triggering mechanism is activated.* Nevertheless, stripped as we show it for the sake of clarity, SYNCHROVEST turned in a creditable performance riding a volatile Fund vehicle through the second worse crash in history, and cruising calmly on the placid NYSE index—ending up not only with a nice profit, but a comfortable bank account as well.

Did you? The wave of redemptions that swept the Mutual Fund industry the following year—and the thick pessimism that settled over empty brokerage houses—indicate that you did not.

Keep in mind that your *Credit Balance* is part of your investment program. These "extra stones" are the stones that will widen the base of your pyramid. Don't fret that the money is just lying there idle. First of all, it's growing at the rate of 5.47%—and many's the year in Wall Street that an investor would be glad to come out ahead 5.47%. Second, as the market soars, it becomes increasingly more vulnerable; and those "idle" dollars are actually growing proportionately stronger both in terms of what they will shortly be able to buy at a discount and the interest they are presently earning! They are the anchor you keep to windward.

You may say yes, but the price of my Mutual Fund that I see in the paper on the last of the month may change considerably in the three or four days it takes for them to get my check. Rarely will the price change considerably in that length of time, and any price change will work as much for you as against you over a period of time. As a matter of fact, since prices tend to plunge faster than they soar, you may find yourself receiving a benefit more often than you pay a penalty. Besides, many of those Fund prices in the papers aren't real prices anyway; they are estimates. Few Funds or the Funds' custodial banks can compute their asset value per share between the Exchange's closing and the 5:00 p.m. deadline the newspapers insist on. Rather than submit a "not available," they'll make an estimate. And now you know why some Funds seem to turn in a sterling performance on a bad day.

One group of Funds, Investors Diversified Services, chooses an alternative. Because it's impossible for them to value their $6 billion portfolio in 90 minutes, they use yesterday's price. Thus, the price of IDS Funds you see in Wednesday morning's paper is Monday's closing price, not Tuesday's.

SYNCHROVEST *automatically* lowers your center of gravity, *automatically* scoops up your security blanket and tucks it around you after you tumble down a step. It is nothing less than a full-time personal investment counselor.

Observe, in our examples, how SYNCHROVEST automatically reaches into your pocket during a falling market and steals fresh funds for your program. Observe the power of those vigorous new funds to round up and bring back weakening shares. In a rising market, that reserve of new funds acts as an automatic check against overenthusiasm. "Somewhere," says Burke, "there must be a control upon will and appetite, and the less of it there is within, the more of it there must be without."

SYNCHROVEST *is* that control.

Finally, since the fearful Dollar Cost Averager tends to abandon his program during a crash—the precise time at which he *must* continue if he is to achieve any sort of result—SYNCHROVEST builds up a cash reserve for use during this critical period. Since the Synchrovestor has already pledged these funds to the market, he will tend to invest them—particularly since the "fun" feature built into SYNCHROVEST makes it enjoyable to do so. This "forced investment" factor alone makes SYNCHROVEST worthy of serious consideration to the disenchanted investor. And the jittery Synchrovestor who *does* jettison his program near the bottom will usually make out far better than the Dollar Cost Averager in a similar position!

There is another valuable dimension to SYNCHROVEST—its use in lump-sum investing. Rather than risk the dangers of decline immediately after investing the lump sum, SYNCHROVEST, recognizing that the market can be roughly divisible into a four-year cycle, suggests that we divide our lump sum into 48 equal parts (48 months). If the resultant parts are too small for practical investment, the lump sum can be divided into 24 or 36 months. The important thing is to avoid committing all of your capital to the market during a period that may later turn out to have been the high and to prepare yourself for the opportunity of benefiting from a possible decline in the future. The Chase Manhattan Paper Portfolio Program, spanning as it did 20 months, required us to divide our $100,000,000 nest-egg into 20 payments of $5,000,000 each. Note that, in lump-sum investing, there is no necessity to build up a *Credit Balance;* the *Credit Balance* is already there. In this case, SYNCHROVEST is used "full strength." *Base Investment* and *Planned Investment* are one and the same: $5,000,000.

NEW YORK STOCK EXCHANGE INDEX

Jan. 31, 1967 - Dec. 31, 1971 (5 years)
DOLLAR COST AVERAGING

		Price	Shares Bought	Shares Owned	Total Inv.
1967	1.	47	6.4	6.4	300
	2.	48	6.3	12.7	600
	3.	50	6.0	18.7	900
	4.	52	5.8	24.5	1,200
	5.	49	6.1	30.6	1,500
	6.	50	6.0	36.6	1,800
	7.	53	5.7	42.3	2,100
	8.	52	5.8	48.1	2,400
	9.	54	5.6	53.7	2,700
	10.	52	5.8	59.5	3,000
	11.	52	5.8	65.3	3,300
	12.	54	5.6	70.9	3,600
1968	1.	52	5.8	76.7	3,900
	2.	50	6.0	82.7	4,200
	3.	50	6.0	88.7	4,500
	4.	54	5.6	94.3	4,800
	5.	56	5.4	99.7	5,100
	6.	56	5.4	105.1	5,400
	7.	55	5.5	110.6	5,700
	8.	55	5.5	116.1	6,000
	9.	58	5.2	121.3	6,300
	10.	58	5.2	126.5	6,600
	11.	61	4.9	131.4	6,900
	12.	59	5,1	136.5	7,200
1969	1.	58	5.2	141.7	7,500
	2.	55	5.5	147.2	7,800
	3.	57	5.3	152.5	8,100
	4.	58	5.2	157.7	8,400
	5.	58	5.2	162.9	8,700
	6.	54	5.6	168.5	9,000
	7.	51	5.9	174.4	9,300
	8.	53	5.7	180.1	9,600
	9.	52	5.8	185.9	9,900
	10.	54	5.6	191.5	10,200
	11.	52	5.8	197.3	10,500
	12.	52	5.8	203.1	10,800

Chart A

NEW YORK STOCK EXCHANGE INDEX

1/31/67 — 12/31/71 (5 years)
DOLLAR COST AVERAGING

		Price	Shares Bought	Shares Owned	Total Inv.
1970	1.	48	6.3	209.4	11,100
	2.	50	6.0	215.4	11,400
	3.	50	6.0	221.4	11,700
	4.	45	6.7	228.1	12,000
	5.	42	7.1	235.2	12,300
*	6.	40	7.5	242.7	12,600
	7.	42	7.1	249.8	12,900
	8.	44	6.8	256.6	13,200
	9.	46	6.5	263.1	13,500
	10.	45	6.7	269.8	13,800
	11.	47	6.4	276.2	14,100
†	12.	50	6.0	282.2	14,400
1971‡	1.	53	5.7	287.9	14,700
	2.	53	5.7	293.6	15,000
	3.	55	5.5	299.1	15,300
	4.	57	5.3	304.4	15,600
	5.	55	5.5	309.9	15,900
	6.	55	5.5	315.4	16,200
	7.	53	5.7	321.1	16,500
	8.	55	5.5	326.6	16,800
	9.	54	5.6	332.2	17,100
	10.	52	5.8	338.0	17,400
	11.	52	5.8	343.8	17,700
	12.	56	5.4	349.2	18,000

FINAL PROFIT: $1,544

*At bottom of market, Dollar Cost has loss of $2,880, SYNCHROVEST a loss of $2,365.

†At this point, Dollar Cost has reduced its *loss* to $300; but SYNCHROVEST now has a profit of $177!

‡Dollar Cost profit: $564. *SYNCHROVEST profit;* $951!

Chart A (cont'd.)

Chart A-1

NEW YORK STOCK EXCHANGE INDEX

1/31/67 - 12/31/71 (5 years)

SYNCHROVEST

		Date	Price	Investment	Shares Bought	Total Shares	Total Investment	Cost Per Share	Credit Balance
1967	*	1.	47	$300*	6.4	6.4	$300	47	0
		2.	48	221	4.6	11.0	521	47	79
		3.	50	212	4.2	15.2	733	49	167
		4.	52	212	4.1	19.3	945	50	255
		5.	49	230 + 5 = 235	4.8	24.1	1,180	49	320
		6.	50	221	4.4	28.5	1,401	48	399
		7.	53	205	3.9	32.4	1,606	50	494
		8.	52	216	4.2	36.6	1,822	49	578
		9.	54	205	3.8	40.4	2,027	51	673
		10.	52	221	4.3	44.7	2,248	50	752
		11.	52	216	4.2	48.9	2,464	50	836
		12.	54	209	3.9	52.8	2,673	50	927
1968		1.	52	216	4.2	57.0	2,889	51	1,011
		2.	50	230 + 23 = 253	5.1	62.1	3,142	51	1,058
		3.	50	230 + 24 = 254	5.1	67.2	3,396	51	1,104
		4.	54	212	3.9	71.1	3,608	51	1,192
		5.	56	205	3.7	74.8	3,813	51	1,287
		6.	56	205	3.7	78.5	4,018	51	1,382
		7.	55	209	3.8	82.3	4,227	52	1,473
		8.	55	214	3.9	86.2	4,441	52	1,559

	9.	58	203	3.5	89.7	4,644	52	1,656
	10.	58	203	3.5	93.2	4,847	52	1,753
	11.	61	191	3.1	96.3	5,038	52	1,862
	12.	59	198	3.4	99.7	5,236	52	1,964
1969	1.	58	203	3.5	103.2	5,439	53	2,061
	2.	55	216	3.9	107.1	5,655	53	2,145
	3.	57	209	3.7	110.8	5,864	53	2,236
	4.	58	205	3.5	114.3	6,069	53	2,331
	5.	58	205	3.5	117.8	6,274	53	2,426
	6.	54	221	4.1	121.9	6,495	53	2,505
	7.	51	234 + 100 = 334	6.5	128.4	6,829	53	2,471
	8.	53	225	4.2	132.6	7,054	53	2,546
	9.	52	230 + 51 = 281	5.4	138.0	7,335	53	2,565
	10.	54	221	4.1	142.1	7,556	53	2,644
	11.	52	230 + 53 = 283	5.4	147.5	7,839	53	2,661
	12.	52	230 + 53 = 283	5.4	152.9	8,122	53	2,678
1970	1.	48	248 + 268 = 516	10.8	163.7	8,638	53	2,462
	2.	50	239 + 148 = 387	7.7	171.4	9,025	53	2,375
	3.	50	239 + 143 = 382	7.6	179.0	9,407	53	2,293
	4.	45	266 + 413 = 679	15.1	194.1	10,086	52	1,914
	5.	42	279 + 459 = 738	17.6	211.7	10,824	51	1,476
	6.	40	288 + 413 = 701	17.5	229.2	11,525	50	1,075
	7.	42	268 + 204 = 472	11.2	240.4	11,997	50	903
	8.	44	257 + 126 = 383	8.7	249.1	12,380	50	820
	9.	46	245 + 74 = 319	6.9	256.0	12,699	50	801
	10.	45	250 + 88 = 338	7.5	263.5	13,037	49	763
	11.	47	234 + 31 = 265	5.6	269.1	13,302	49	798
	12.	50	221	4.4	273.5	13,523	49	877

(cont'd.)

Chart A-1 (cont'd.)

NEW YORK STOCK EXCHANGE INDEX

1/31/67 - 12/31/71 (5 years)

SYNCHROVEST

	Date	Price	Investment	Shares Bought	Total Shares	Total Investment	Cost Per Share	Credit Balance
1971	1.	53	207	3.9	277.4	13,730	50	970
	2.	53	212	4.0	281.4	13,942	50	1,058
	3.	55	205	3.7	285.1	14,147	50	1,153
	4.	57	198	3.5	288.6	14,345	50	1,255
	5.	55	205	3.7	292.3	14,550	50	1,350
	6.	55	205	3.7	296.0	14,755	50	1,445
	7.	53	212	4.0	300.0	14,967	50	1,533
	8.	55	205	3.7	303.7	15,172	50	1,628
	9.	54	209	3.9	307.6	15,381	50	1,719
	10.	52	216	4.2	311.8	15,597	50	1,803
	11.	52	216	4.2	316.0	15,813	50	1,887
	12.	56	200	3.6	319.6	16,013		1,987

FINAL PROFIT: $1,907 + bank interest

*Because most investment programs require an initial investment somewhat higher than the typical investor's subsequent monthly investments, our SYNCHROVEST charts assume an initial investment identical to Dollar Cost Averager's.

Ideally, a separate bank account should be used for each stock being accumulated with SYNCHROVEST, but this may prove impractical and unwieldy for those who wish to maintain a number of such programs. An excellent compromise would be to use a *single* bank account to hold all reserve funds for every stock being accumulated. There will be no confusion as to how much of the *Credit Balance* belongs to Stock A and how much to Stock B if proper records are kept on each stock. As has been indicated, the final column on your record sheet for each stock contains the running total of your *Credit Balance.* A glance at this column tells you immediately how much reserve money you have in the bank that has been earmarked for this particular stock.

A single bank account, then, offers us the simplicity and convenience to enable us to maintain an unlimited number of SYNCHROVEST accounts. The only "drawback" to such an arrangement is the interest that will accumulate on the bank account. To which stock does the interest belong? How much of it belongs to Stock A, how much to Stock B, etc.?

It seems eminently practicable to divide the interest into equal amounts and credit each of your stock records with the same amount of money. Once every quarter, your bank will enter interest in your passbook. Assume it is $90. If you have two SYNCHROVEST programs going, divide two into $90. That gives you $45. Simply increase the *Credit Balance* on each of your two record sheets by $45. Granted, Stock A's *Credit Balance* may not actually have earned $45; and Stock B's *Credit Balance* may, in fact, have earned *more* than $45. But in the final analysis, this communal arrangement should yield quite satisfactory results. For one thing, in the subsequent quarter, Stock A's *Credit Balance* may earn more than $45 while Stock B's may not! Why? Because the *Credit Balance* will fluctuate. Money may flow into the account from Stock A's investment program, and money may flow out of the account if Stock B's investment program demands it. The natural ebb and flow of funds through your bank account should result in a fairly even distribution of interest all around over a period of time. But even if it does not, even if Stock A, for example, undeservedly ends up with the lion's share of the interest, who is to say that Stock A will not make better use of it than Stock B? All things being equal, it probably *will* do so; for if Stock B has built up a larger *Credit Balance* and thus earned more interest, it means that the price of Stock B has been climbing more rapidly. In a subsequent market plunge, it may not decline sufficiently to permit much triggering of its reserves. Stock A, which has not been building up reserves at the same pace, has obviously not risen in price as much and is hovering closer to its triggering point.

We said, "All things being equal," creating the impression that the Stock A program and the Stock B program were begun at the same time and with the same *Planned Investments.* But even if the Stock B program was begun months or even years after the Stock A program, and even if its *Planned Investment* was half that of the Stock A program, there is still no way of knowing which stock will make the most effective use of its interest allotment. It should be of little concern to the SYNCHROVESTOR *which* stock is treated fairly or unfairly in the interest distribution. His dreams swirl about a market skid that will trigger *all* his stocks and squeeze them dry of *all* their reserves. But he will be pleased if at least one stock performed that way—and that stock could very well turn out to be the one that received more interest than it was entitled to.

Remember, we are not talking about the all-important *Credit Balance.* Each stock has its own exact *Credit Balance,* and not a penny of it is shared with any other stock. We are speaking of the *interest* on these funds—"found money," if you will. It is another bonus to you for using SYNCHROVEST. Your SYNCHROVEST programs may or may not ever ask you to invest it. If it does, you will make out like a bandit when the market turns around. And if it doesn't, it's still there, a treasure chest growing heftier by the hour.

ROWE PRICE NEW HORIZONS FUND

1/31/67 — 12/31/71 (5 years)

Dollar Cost Averaging

		Price	Shares Bought	Shares Owned	Total Inv.
1967	1.	17.16	17.5	17.5	300
	2.	18.10	16.6	34.1	600
	3.	19.51	15.4	49.5	900
	4.	20.94	14.3	63.8	1,200
	5.	20.52	14.6	78.4	1,500
	6.	22.26	13.5	91.9	1,800
	7.	23.81	12.6	104.5	2,100
	8.	23.71	12.7	117.2	2,400
	9.	25.83	11.6	128.8	2,700
	10.	25.79	11.6	140.4	3,000
	11.	26.83	11.2	151.6	3,300
	Dist:	$240	8.9	160.5	3,540
	12.	26.97	11.1	171.6	3,840
1968	1.	25.37	11.8	183.4	4,140
	2.	23.78	12.6	196.0	4,440
	3.	24.01	12.5	208.5	4,740
	4.	27.99	10.7	219.2	5,040
	5.	29.89	10.0	229.2	5,340
	6.	29.69	10.1	239.3	5,640
	7.	28.25	10.6	249.9	5,940
	8.	29.71	10.1	260.0	6,240
	9.	31.52	9.5	269.5	6,540
	10.	31.95	9.4	278.9	6,840
	11.	33.52	8.9	287.8	7,140
	12.	33.24	9.0	296.8	7,440
1969	1.	30.36	9.9	306.7	7,740
	Dist:	$564	18.6	325.3	8,304
	2.	28.19	10.6	335.9	8,604
	3.	28.59	10.5	346.4	8,904
	4.	29.33	10.2	356.6	9,204
	5.	29.82	10.1	366.7	9,504
	6.	27.34	11.0	377.7	9,804
	7.	25.04	12.0	389.7	10,104
	8.	26.80	11.2	400.9	10,404
	9.	27.28	11.0	411.9	10,704
	10.	29.76	10.1	422.0	11,004
	11.	29.02	10.3	432.3	11,304
	12.	29.15	10.3	442.6	11,604

Chart B

ROWE PRICE NEW HORIZONS FUND

1/31/67 — 12/31/71 (5 years)

Dollar Cost Averaging

			Price	Shares Bought	Shares Owned	Total Inv.
1970		1.	26.11	11.5	454.1	11,904
		Dist:	$625	23.9	478.0	12,529
		2.	26.74	11.2	489.2	12,829
		3.	25.53	11.8	501.0	13,129
		4.	20.78	14.4	515.4	13,428
		5.	19.00	15.8	531.2	13,729
	*	6.	18.31	16.4	547.6	14,029
		7.	19.47	15.4	563.0	14,329
		8.	20.34	14.7	577.7	14,629
		9.	22.54	13.3	591.0	14,929
		10.	22.03	13.6	604.6	15,229
		11.	22.83	13.1	617.7	15,529
		12.	24.36	12.3	630.0	15,829
1971	†	1.	25.05	12.0	642.0	16,129
		Dist:	$391	15.1	657.1	16,520
		2.	26.35	11.4	668.5	16,820
		3.	28.42	10.6	679.1	17,120
		4.	29.25	10.3	689.4	17,420
		5.	28.86	10.4	699.8	17,720
		6.	29.96	10.0	709.8	18,020
		7.	29.00	10.3	720.1	18,320
		8.	31.23	9.6	729.7	18,620
		9.	32.37	9.3	739.0	18,920
		10.	31.26	9.6	748.6	19,220
	‡	11.	31.76	9.4	758.0	19,520
		12.	36.19	8.3	766.3	19,820

FINAL PROFIT: $7,902

---

*At bottom of market, Dollar Cost has loss of $3,995, SYNCHROVEST a loss of $2,738.

†At this point, Dollar Cost has reduced its *loss* to $47, but SYNCHROVEST now has a *profit* of $1,099!

‡Profit at this point, Dollar Cost $4,554, SYNCHROVEST $5,460!

Chart B (cont'd.)

Chart B-1

ROWE PRICE NEW HORIZONS FUND

1/31/67 - 12/31/71 (5 years)

SYNCHROVEST

	Date	Price	Investment	Shares Bought	Total Shares	Total Investment	Cost Per Share	Credit Balance
1967	1.	17.16	$300	17.5	17.5	$300	17	0
	2.	18.10	212	11.7	29.2	512	18	88
	3.	19.51	203	10.4	39.6	715	18	185
	4.	20.94	194	9.3	48.9	909	19	291
	5.	20.52	203	9.9	58.8	1,112	19	388
	6.	22.26	194	8.7	67.5	1,306	19	494
	7.	23.81	178	7.5	75.0	1,484	20	616
	8.	23.71	187	7.9	82.9	1,671	20	729
	9.	25.83	173	6.7	89.6	1,844	20	856
	10.	25.79	173	6.7	96.3	2,017	21	983
	11.	26.83	176	6.6	102.9	2,193	21	1,107
	Dist:	27.06	163	6.0	108.9	2,356	22	1,107
	12.	26.97	182	6.7	115.6	2,538	22	1,225
1968	1.	25.37	198	7.8	123.4	2,736	22	1,327
	2.	23.78	207	8.7	132.1	2,943	22	1,420
	3.	24.01	207	8.6	140.7	3,150	22	1,513
	4.	27.99	178	6.4	147.1	3,328	23	1,635
	5.	29.89	173	5.8	152.9	3,501	23	1,762
	6.	29.69	173	5.8	158.7	3,674	23	1,889
	7.	28.25	185	6.5	165.2	3,859	23	2,004
	8.	29.71	173	5.8	171.0	4,032	24	2,131

	9.	31.52	169	5.4	176.4	4,201	24	2,262
	10.	31.95	169	5.3	181.7	4,370	24	2,393
	11.	33.52	160	4.8	186.5	4,530	24	2,533
	12.	33.24	164	4.9	191.4	4,694	25	2,669
1969	1.	30.36	187	6.2	197.6	4,881		2,782
	Dist:	30.29	363	12.0	209.6	5,244	25	2,782
	2.	28.19	200	7.1	216.7	5,444	25	2,882
	3.	28.59	194	6.8	223.5	5,638	25	2,988
	4.	29.33	194	6.6	230.1	5,832	25	3,094
	5.	29.82	187	6.3	236.4	6,019	26	3,207
	6.	27.34	216	7.9	244.3	6,235	26	3,291
	7.	25.04	234 + 132 = 366	14.6	258.9	6,601	25	3,225
	8.	26.80	209	7.8	266.7	6,810	26	3,316
	9.	27.28	216	7.9	274.6	7,026	26	3,400
	10.	29.76	196	6.6	281.2	7,222	26	3,504
	11.	29.02	203	7.0	288.2	7,425	26	3,601
	12.	29.15	203	7.0	295.2	7,628	26	3,698
1970	1.	26.11	225	8.6	303.8	7,853		3,773
	Dist:	26.13	416	15.9	319.7	8,269	26	3,773
	2.	26.74	216	8.1	327.8	8,485	26	3,857
	3.	25.53	225	8.8	336.6	8,710	26	3,932
	4.	20.78	279 + 944 = 1223	58.9	395.5	9,933	25	3,009
	5.	19.00	297 + 963 = 1260	66.3	461.8	11,193	24	2,049
	6.	18.31	299 + 676 = 975	53.2	515.0	12,168	24	1,374
	7.	19.47	284 + 357 = 641	32.9	547.9	12,809	23	1,033
	8.	20.34	259 + 155 = 414	20.4	568.3	13,223	23	919
	9.	22.54	225	10.0	578.3	13,448	23	994
	10.	22.03	236 + 50 = 286	13.0	591.3	13,734	23	1,008
	11.	22.83	225	9.9	601.2	13,959	23	1,083
	12.	24.36	216	8.9	610.1	14,175	23	1,167

(cont'd.)

ROWE PRICE NEW HORIZONS FUND

1/31/67 - 12/31/71 (5 years)

SYNCHROVEST

	Date	Price	Investment	Shares Bought	Total Shares	Total Investment	Cost Per Share	Credit Balance
1971	1.	25.05	207	8.3	618.4	14,382		1,260
	Dist:	25.96	378	14.6	633.0	14,760	23	1,260
	2.	26.35	198	7.5	640.5	14,958	23	1,362
	3.	28.42	185	6.5	647.0	15,143	23	1,477
	4.	29.25	178	6.1	653.1	15,321	23	1,599
	5.	28.86	178	6.2	659.3	15,499	24	1,721
	6.	29.96	180	6.0	665.3	15,679	24	1,841
	7.	29.00	187	6.4	671.7	15,866	24	1,954
	8.	31.23	173	5.5	677.2	16,039	24	2,081
	9.	32.37	169	5.2	682.4	16,208	24	2,212
	10.	31.26	173	5.5	687.9	16,381	24	2,339
	11.	31.76	169	5.3	693.2	16,550	24	2,470
	12.	36.19	151	4.2	697.4	16,701		2,619

FINAL PROFIT: $8,523 + bank interest

Chart B-1 (cont'd.)

Chart C

ROWE PRICE NEW HORIZONS FUND

Results if investors had begun investment program at top of market, 11/68, using Dollar Cost Averaging

			Price	Shares Bought	Shares Owned	Total Inv.
1968		11.	33.52	8.9	8.9	300
		12.	33.24	9.0	17.9	600
1969		1.	30.36	9.9	27.8	900
		Dist:	$34	1.1	28.9	934
		2.	28.19	10.6	39.5	1,234
		3.	28.59	10.5	50.0	1,534
		4.	29.33	10.2	60.2	1,834
		5.	29.82	10.1	70.3	2,134
		6.	27.34	11.0	81.3	2,434
		7.	25.04	12.0	93.3	2,734
		8.	26.80	11.2	104.5	3,034
		9.	27.28	11.0	115.5	3,334
		10.	29.76	10.1	125.6	3,634
		11.	29.02	10.3	135.9	3,934
		12.	29.15	10.3	146.2	4,234
1970		1.	26.11	11.5	157.7	4,534
		Dist:	$206	7.9	165.6	4,740
		2.	26.74	11.2	176.8	5,040
		3.	25.53	11.8	188.6	5,340
		4.	20.78	14.4	203.0	5,640
		5.	19.00	15.8	218.8	5,940
	*	6.	18.31	16.4	235.2	6,240
		7.	19.47	15.4	250.6	6,540
		8.	20.34	14.7	265.3	6,840
		9.	22.54	13.3	278.6	7,140
		10.	22.03	13.6	292.2	7,440
		11.	22.83	13.1	305.3	7,740
		12.	24.36	12.3	317.6	8,040
1971	†	1.	25.05	12.0	329.6	8,340
		Dist:	$197	7.6	337.2	8,537
		2.	26.35	11.4	348.6	8,837
		3.	28.42	10.6	359.2	9,137
		4.	29.25	10.3	369.5	9,437
		5.	28.86	10.4	379.9	9,737
		6.	29.96	10.0	389.9	10,037
		7.	29.00	10.3	400.2	10,337
		8.	31.23	9.6	409.8	10,637
		9.	32.37	9.3	419.1	10,937
		10.	31.26	9.6	428.7	11,237
	‡	11.	31.76	9.4	438.1	11,537
		12.	36.19	8.3	446.4	11,837

FINAL PROFIT: $4,304

*At bottom of market, Dollar Cost has loss of $1,937, SYNCHROVEST a loss of $1,718. Price of stock has fallen 45% from its high.

†At this point, Dollar Cost has cut its *loss* to $73, but SYNCHROVEST has a *profit* of $154!

‡Profit at this point, Dollar Cost $2,374, SYNCHROVEST $2,493!

Chart C-1

ROWE PRICE NEW HORIZONS FUND

Results if investor had begun investment program at top of market, 11/68, using SYNCHROVEST:

	Date	Price	Investment	Shares Bought	Total Shares	Total Investment	Cost Per Share	Credit Balance
1968	11.	33.52	$300	8.9	8.9	$300	34	0
	12.	33.24	232	7.0	15.9	532	33	68
1969	1.	30.36	248 + 7 = 255	8.4	24.3	787		113
	Dist:	30.29	30	1.0	25.3	817	33	113
	2.	28.19	266 + 20 = 286	10.1	35.4	1,103	32	127
	3.	28.59	248 + 13 = 261	9.1	44.5	1,364	30	166
	4.	29.33	232 + 5 = 237	8.1	52.6	1,601	30	229
	5.	29.82	225	7.5	60.1	1,826	30	304
	6.	27.34	250 + 33 = 283	10.4	70.5	2,109	30	321
	7.	25.04	270 + 64 = 334	13.3	83.8	2,443	29	287
	8.	26.80	241 + 20 = 261	9.7	93.5	2,704	29	326
	9.	27.28	241 + 23 = 264	9.7	103.2	2,968	29	362
	10.	29.76	218	7.3	110.5	3,186	29	444
	11.	29.02	225	7.8	118.3	3,411	29	519
	12.	29.15	225	7.7	126.0	3,636	29	594
1970	1.	26.11	252 + 71 = 323	12.4	138.4	3,959		571
	Dist:	26.13	178	6.8	145.2	4,137	29	571
	2.	26.74	241 + 40 = 281	10.5	155.7	4,418	28	590

	3.	25.53	243 + 47 = 290	11.4	167.1	4,708	28	600
	4.	20.78	299 + 198 = 497	23.9	191.0	5,205	27	403
	5.	19.00	320 + 169 = 489	25.7	216.7	5,694	26	214
	6.	18.31	324 + 94 = 418	22.8	239.5	6,112	25	96
	7.	19.47	297 + 31 = 328	16.8	256.3	6,440	25	68
	8.	20.34	281 + 17 = 298	14.7	271.0	6,738	25	70
	9.	22.54	245 + 6 = 251	11.1	282.1	6,989	25	119
	10.	22.03	257 + 17 = 274	12.4	294.5	7,263	25	145
	11.	22.83	245 + 13 = 258	11.3	305.8	7,521	25	187
	12.	24.36	234 + 7 = 241	9.9	315.7	7,762	25	246
1971	1.	25.05	225	9.0	324.7	7,987		321
	Dist:	25.96	196	7.6	332.3	8,183	25	321
	2.	26.35	216	8.2	340.5	8,399	25	405
	3.	28.42	200	7.0	347.5	8,599	25	505
	4.	29.25	194	6.6	354.1	8,793	25	611
	5.	28.86	194	6.7	360.8	8,987	25	717
	6.	29.96	187	6.2	367.0	9,174	25	830
	7.	29.00	194	6.7	373.7	9,368	25	936
	8.	31.23	182	5.8	379.5	9,550	25	1,054
	9.	32.37	176	5.4	384.9	9,726	25	1,178
	10.	31.26	182	5.8	390.7	9,908	25	1,296
	11.	31.76	176	5.5	396.2	10,084	25	1,420
	12.	36.19	155	4.3	400.5	10,239		1,565

FINAL PROFIT: $4,273 + bank interest

One day during the course of your SYNCHROVEST program, SYNCHROVEST may call for an investment that is *half* of your original *Planned Investment.* Magically, this is SYNCHROVEST'S way of informing you that you now have a profit of 50% on all your invested money, not counting your bank interest, and that it is time to begin building a larger pyramid. (Did not the great Leonardo himself tell us that "one pyramid passes through the other without confusion"?) This is done simply by converting your *Base Investment* into your *Planned Investment.* Your *Base Investment,* remember, was only 75% of your *Planned Investment.* Now that you have built up a substantial *Credit Balance,* it is not nearly as necessary to build up reserves as it was in the beginning.

Using your *Planned Investment,* you will continue to add to your reserves automatically in a rising market, but at a reduced rate—while bank interest on your *Credit Balance* is swelling your reserves at an accelerated rate!

To make this perfectly clear, imagine that you began your SYNCHROVEST program with a *Planned Investment* of $100 a month. Your *Base Investment* would have been 75% of that, or $75.00. This was the figure you would have been using in your calculations all along. Today, the *Price Per Share* of your stock is $30.00, and your *Cost Per Share* is $20.00. As you do every month, you divide the *Price Per Share* into the *Cost Per Share.* The result here is .67. Finally, you multiply .67 by your *Base Investment,* $75.00, to find out how much SYNCHROVEST wants you to invest. The answer is $50.00—which is exactly half of your original *Planned Investment* of $100.00.

You may break open a bottle of champagne to celebrate—and then you may wash and dry your *Base Investment* and store it away in a drawer someplace. You won't need it anymore.

You now blow the dust off your *Planned Investment,* $100,

and use *that* figure in future computations. Do it now. Mutliply .67 by $100.00 and you will see that SYNCHROVEST has upped the ante. It wants you to invest $67.00—34% more than the old figure of $50.00.

SYNCHROVEST has steered you carefully out of the harbor and into the open sea.

It is a question of philosophy whether it would be better at this point simply to "cash in" and start all over again with a new *Cost Per Share.* With the price of the stock now 50% higher than your *Cost Per Share,* you may reason that the stock is unlikely to go all the way back down below your *Cost Per Share* and trigger your fat *Credit Balance* so that you can accumulate large numbers of cheap shares. Before making your decision, remember that you don't need a drop of 50% here before your reserves are triggered, but only a slump of 33⅓%! A $30.00 stock that declines to $20.00 has lost 33⅓%—and in today's volatile market, that's hardly far-fetched. (In the first six months of 1973 alone, various broad-based averages showed a similar decline in the market, with many individual stocks and Mutual Funds suffering a more severe price erosion.) Remember, too, that your 50% profit is only temporary. Each subsequent purchase up here *raises* your *Cost Per Share* and increases the likelihood of triggering your *Credit Balance.* Even if the stock stands still, your continued purchases at this level are not only putting you in a position to make greater profits, but by raising your *Cost Per Share* are increasing the possibility that your swollen *Credit Balance* will be triggered.

Mutual Fund owners should also bear in mind that huge capital gains distributions are made at the top of a market, and that these sometimes massive amounts of capital buying high-priced shares can have an energizing effect on the *Cost Per Share,* nudging it significantly upward and improving the odds that your *Credit Balance* will be triggered. Capital gains distributions at these price levels thus act to "prime" the SYNCHROVEST mechanism.

We have seen that SYNCHROVEST allows us to make a profit of 50% before flashing a signal for us to shift gears from *Base Investment* to *Planned Investment.* Mutual Fund owners and other investors who have their distributions reinvested automatically will realize immediately that they have, in fact, earned much more than 50% when the light flashes. How? Because their *Cost Per Share* reflects purchases made by dividend and capital gains distributions as well as out-of-pocket money and is therefore *higher* than their actual out-of-pocket *Cost Per Share.* They might thus, for example, have a real profit closer to 100% than to 50%.

DOW JONES INDUSTRIAL AVERAGE

Jan. 31, 1967 - Dec. 31, 1971 (5 years)

Dollar Cost Averaging

Date	Price	Investment	Shares Bought	Shares Owned	Total Investment
1/67	850	$300	.353	.353	$300
2/67	839	$300	.358	.711	$600
3/67	866	$300	.346	1.057	$900
4/67	897	$300	.334	1.391	$1,200
5/67	853	$300	.352	1.743	$1,500
6/67	860	$300	.349	2.092	$1,800
7/67	904	$300	.332	2.424	$2,100
8/67	901	$300	.333	2.757	$2,400
9/67	927	$300	.324	3.081	$2,700
10/67	880	$300	.341	3.422	$3,000
11/67	876	$300	.342	3.764	$3,300
12/67	905	$300	.331	4.095	$3,600
1/68	855	$300	.351	4.446	$3,900
2/68	841	$300	.357	4.803	$4,200
3/68	841	$300	.357	5.160	$4,500
4/68	912	$300	.329	5.489	$4,800
5/68	899	$300	.334	5.823	$5,100
6/68	898	$300	.334	6.157	$5,400
7/68	883	$300	.340	6.497	$5,700
8/68	896	$300	.335	6.832	$6,000
9/68	936	$300	.321	7.153	$6,300
10/68	952	$300	.315	7.468	$6,600
11/68	985	$300	.305	7.773	$6,900
12/68	944	$300	.318	8.091	$7,200
1/69	946	$300	.317	8.408	$7,500
2/69	905	$300	.331	8.739	$7,800
3/69	935	$300	.321	9.060	$8,100
4/69	950	$300	.316	9.376	$8,400
5/69	938	$300	.320	9.696	$8,700
5/69	873	$300	.344	10.040	$9,000
7/69	815	$300	.368	10.408	$9,300
8/69	837	$300	.358	10.766	$9,600
9/69	813	$300	.369	11.135	$9,900
10/69	856	$300	.350	11.485	$10,200
11/69	812	$300	.369	11.854	$10,500
12/69	800	$300	.375	12.229	$10,800

Chart D

DOW JONES INDUSTRIAL AVERAGE

Jan. 31, 1967 - Dec. 31, 1971 (5 years)

Dollar Cost Averaging

Date	Price	Investment	Shares Bought	Shares Owned	Total Investment
1/70	744	$300	.403	12.632	$11,100
2/70	778	$300	.386	13,018	$11,400
3/70	786	$300	.382	13.400	$11,700
4/70	736	$300	.408	13.808	$12,000
5/70	700	$300	.429	14.237	$12,300
6/70	684	$300	.439	14.676	$12,600
7/70	734	$300	.409	15.085	$12,900
8/70	765	$300	.392	15.477	$13,200
9/70	761	$300	.394	15.871	$13,500
10/70	756	$300	.397	16.268	$13,800
11/70	794	$300	.378	16.646	$14,100
12/70	839	$300	.358	17.004	$14,400
1/71	869	$300	.345	17.349	$14,700
2/71	879	$300	.341	17.690	$15,000
3/71	904	$300	.332	18.022	$15,300
4/71	942	$300	.318	18.340	$15,600
5/71	908	$300	.330	18.670	$15,900
6/71	891	$300	.337	19.007	$16,200
7/71	858	$300	.350	19.357	$16,500
8/71	898	$300	.334	19.691	$16,800
9/71	887	$300	.338	20.029	$17,100
10/71	839	$300	.358	20.387	$17,400
11/71	831	$300	.361	20.748	$17,700
12/71	890	$300	.337	21.085	$18,000

FINAL PROFIT: $766

Chart D (cont'd.)

Chart D-1

DOW JONES INDUSTRIAL AVERAGE

Jan. 31, 1967 - Dec. 31, 1971 (5 years)

SYNCHROVEST

Date	Price	Investment	Shares Bought	Shares Owned	Total Investment	Cost Per Share	Credit Balance
1/67	850	$300	.353	.353	$300	850	0
2/67	839	227	.271	.624	527	845	73
3/67	866	221	.255	.879	748	851	152
4/67	897	212	.236	1.115	960	861	240
5/67	853	227 + 2 = 229	.268	1.383	1,189	860	311
6/67	860	225	.262	1.645	1,414	860	386
7/67	904	216	.239	1.884	1,630	865	470
8/67	901	218	.242	2.126	1,848	869	552
9/67	927	212	.229	2.355	2,060	875	640
10/67	880	225	.256	2.611	2,285	875	715
11/67	876	225	.257	2.868	2,510	875	790
12/67	905	218	.241	3.109	2,728	877	872
1/68	855	230 + 17 = 247	.289	3.398	2,975	876	925
2/68	841	236 + 46 = 282	.335	3.733	3,257	872	943
3/68	841	234 + 38 = 272	.323	4.056	3,529	870	971
4/68	912	216	.237	4.293	3,745	872	1,055
5/68	899	218	.242	4.535	3,963	874	1,137
6/68	898	218	.243	4.778	4,181	875	1,219

7/68	883	225	.255	5.033	4,406	875	1,294
8/68	896	221	.247	5.280	4,627	876	1,373
9/68	936	212	.226	5.506	4,839	879	1,461
10/68	952	209	.220	5.726	5,048	882	1,552
11/68	985	200	.203	5.929	5,248	885	1,652
12/68	944	214	.227	6.156	5,462	887	1,738
1/69	946	212	.224	6.380	5,674	889	1,826
2/69	905	221	.244	6.624	5,895	890	1,905
3/69	935	214	.229	6.853	6,109	891	1,991
4/69	950	212	.223	7.076	6,321	893	2,079
5/69	938	214	.228	7.304	6,535	895	2,165
6/69	873	232 + 65 = 297	.340	7.644	6,832	894	2,168
7/69	815	245 + 195 = 440	.540	8.184	7,272	889	2,028
8/69	837	239 + 122 = 361	.431	8.615	7,633	886	1,967
9/69	813	248 + 197 = 445	.547	9.162	8,078	882	1,822
10/69	856	230 + 36 = 266	.311	9.473	8,344	881	1,856
11/69	812	245 + 167 = 412	.507	9.980	8,756	877	1,744
12/69	800	248 + 174 = 422	.528	10.508	9,178	873	1,622
1/70	744	266 + 292 = 558	.750	11.258	9,736	865	1,364
2/70	778	252 + 164 = 416	.535	11.793	10,152	861	1,248
3/70	786	245 + 112 = 357	.454	12.247	10,509	858	1,191
4/70	736	261 + 191 = 452	.614	12.861	10,961	852	1,039
5/70	700	272 + 218 = 490	.700	13.561	11,451	844	849
6/70*	684	279 + 204 = 483	.706	14.267	11,934	836	666
7/70	734	259 + 100 = 359	.489	14.756	12,293	833	607
8/70	765	243 + 49 = 292	.382	15.138	12,585	831	615
9/70	761	245 + 55 = 300	.394	15.532	12,885	830	615

(cont'd.)

Chart D-1 (cont'd.)

DOW JONES INDUSTRIAL AVERAGE

Jan. 31, 1967 - Dec. 31, 1971 (5 years)

SYNCHROVEST

Date	Price	Investment	Shares Bought	Shares Owned	Total Investment	Cost Per Share	Credit Balance
10/70	756	245 + 55 = 300	.397	15.929	13,185	828	615
11/70	794	236 + 31 = 267	.336	16.265	13,452	827	648
†12/70	839	223	.266	16.531	13,675	827	725
1/71	869	214	.246	16.777	13,889	828	811
2/71	879	212	.241	17.018	14,101	829	899
3/71	904	207	.229	17.247	14,308	830	992
4/71	942	198	.210	17.457	14,506	831	1,094
5/71	908	205	.226	17.683	14,711	832	1,189
6/71	891	209	.235	17.918	14,920	833	1,280
7/71	858	218	.254	18.172	15,138	833	1,362
8/71	898	207	.231	18.403	15,345	834	1,455
9/71	887	209	.236	18.639	15,554	834	1,546
10/71	839	223	.266	18.905	15,777	835	1,623
11/71	831	227 + 16 = 243	.292	19.197	16,020	835	1,680
12/71	890	212	.238	19.435	16,232		1,768

FINAL PROFIT: $1,065 + bank interest

*Loss at bottom of market, Dollar Cost Averager $2,562, SYNCHROVEST $2,175.

†At this point, Dollar Cost Averager has a loss of $134, SYNCHROVEST a *profit* of $195!

As an illustration of the explosive difference a bank account can make in your SYNCHROVEST program, imagine that 1% interest has been added quarterly to the *Credit Balance* in Chart D-1 as a rough approximation of a 4% per annum savings account. At the conclusion of the program, SYNCHROVEST's profit becomes $1,339 versus Dollar Cost's $766! Without bank interest, SYNCHROVEST earned 39% more dollar profit than Dollar Cost Averaging, and with far less money invested. With interest, SYNCHROVEST earned 75% more dollar profit than Dollar Cost Averaging! Bank interest not only supplied profit on its own, but allowed larger investments in a falling market.

PROFIT SUPERIORITY OVER
DOLLAR COST AVERAGING

SYNCHROVEST (without interest)
$299 (Actual Profit $1065)

SYNCHROVEST (with interest)
$573 (Actual Profit $1339)

And in December 1970, with Dollar Cost Averaging still nursing a loss to the tune of $134, SYNCHROVEST is gloating over a $400 profit!

Some Mutual Funds may look upon SYNCHROVEST with jaundiced eye; they *like* a heavy cash flow coming in at the top of the market because it "keeps the horse race going" and helps to propel them forward in the performance derby. Some stockbrokers, too, who enjoy their fat commissions during market booms, may view SYNCHROVEST with alarm. But theirs would be a short-range outlook, for the stock market and investors alike have not yet recovered from the excesses of the sixties. In the long run, SYNCHROVEST may represent the salvation of the investment industry. It could keep afloat a Fund that might otherwise go under in crisis; indeed, given wide use, it could even prop up the entire stock market if billions of dollars stood ever poised to rush in and support sagging prices!

We have seen how SYNCHROVEST forces each dollar to work harder. In the foregoing Dow Jones charts, for example, SYNCHROVEST soundly trounced Dollar Cost Averaging with far less money invested. To accomplish this, SYNCHROVEST had to increase the investor's profit percentage on money invested—7% versus 4% for Dollar Cost. The comparison cannot by any means be considered complete, however, for bank interest on SYNCHROVEST's *Credit Balance* has not been taken into consideration. This advantage cannot be stressed too strongly, for if a stock has passed through a 50% decline and is now selling at twice its low, each dollar invested at its low has now doubled! And, as has been shown, SYNCHROVEST makes its largest investments near the bottom. *So we have doubled not only our Credit Balance dollars, but the dollars we have received in interest on that Credit Balance!*

Not a single penny of your *Credit Balance* will ever be used by SYNCHROVEST for any purpose other than to reduce your *Cost Per Share* and increase your profit potential. Remember that every dollar you invest in a stock that is selling at a price higher than your *Cost Per Share* increases your *Cost Per Share* and increases your risk of loss! SYNCHROVEST withdraws from its *Credit Balance* only to make a bargain purchase when the price of the stock is selling at a discount from the investor's *Cost Per Share!* The Dollar Cost Averager, by contrast, invests the same amount of money as the market soars, buying fewer and fewer shares and raising his *Cost Per Share* to a point where a small decline is often sufficient to wipe out painfully acquired profits—or turn a profit into a loss in the twinkling of an eye.

Stock averages, because they are composites of many stocks, tend to flatten out the normal ups and downs of the individual stocks that make them up over the course of a year.

We can suspect, therefore, that the five-year illustrations we have used with these averages—one large decline followed by a recovery—would be duplicated in a one-year period if the investor had chosen an individual security instead. Thus, each decline would offer the opportunity of oomph-asizing his advantage over Dollar Cost—purchasing ever-more-massive amounts of stock with ever-more-massive funds from his *Credit Balance.*

Short of taking a stock down to its low and keeping it there, there is nothing they can do to stop us now. If they are ever to lure buyers into the market, they *must* make the stock fluctuate; and if the stock fluctuates, SYNCHROVEST will pounce. Perhaps that's what Bernard Baruch meant when he was asked what the market was going to do. "It will fluctuate," the great speculator replied with a twinkle in his eye.

In many ways, the following chart is the most fascinating of all, for it shows SYNCHROVEST in mortal combat with all the forces of evil it is ever likely to face. It features the complete and utter collapse of a leveraged Go-Go Mutual Fund in the most recent market carnage, and if it was not the most disappointing performer during this period, only one or two others could claim that distinction. Mercifully, we shall call this Fund the "Amakudari" Fund which, in Japanese, translates loosely as "fallen angels"—for, when the flying was good, nobody flew higher than Amakudari. Unfortunately, its excellent management was abruptly overwhelmed by a variety of insuperable and unprecedented assaults in the '70 crash, not the least of which was the halt in trading of one of its largest holdings that subsequently plunged in value, and the near-panic of the Fund's shareholders to liquidate their holdings. Many other Funds suffered similar problems.

When first plugged in at the fund's inception, SYNCHROVEST hummed and purred in typical "I've got everything under control" fashion, gradually reducing its investments and putting a few dollars in the bank as the stock soared. Then, before SYNCHROVEST had had a chance to build up substantial reserves, it happened. Amakudari, wings riddled, faltered in mid-flight, looped through its contrails of mica dust, and nosedived an incredible 69% downward. SYNCHROVEST's sensitive, advanced circuitry reacted automatically, accelerating its investments and making hasty withdrawals from the bank.

You will note on the chart that an inkling of what was coming occurred at the price of $6.32 on 5/70. SYNCHROVEST's exclusive Overload Protection refused to allow a request for an investment of *all* its bank reserves, instead imposing a ceiling of 50% on such demands as is its custom. (In calculating percentages of bank reserves to be invested by dropping the first digit, all original figures above 1.50 are read as 50%.) This device kept the bank window open for two more months—and then, at the price of $5.57, the window was slammed on SYNCHROVEST'S fingers. The smile vanished from the friendly banker's face as he repossessed your free electric clock (from the company that makes things that go bump in the night). In actual practice, however, accumulated bank interest on SYNCHROVEST's reserves would have kept the window open longer, or permitted larger purchases at this critical time.

What did SYNCHROVEST do? Did it immediately apply for a government subsidy? Not on your floating decimal it didn't. Realizing it had been whipsawed, SYNCHROVEST behaved exactly as a cat does when its foot is held. It did not struggle futilely. Tail thrashing furiously, it stared yellow-eyed at its tormentor, jerked once or twice to test the situation, and then patiently waited for the grip to relax. At the slightest easement of pressure, SYNCHROVEST jerked free.

Then, near the bottom of the market, when reason, logic, and all that's holy dictate maximal investment, SYNCHRO-

VEST deposited a pitiful $3 in the bank! More puzzling still, as the price creeps upward, SYNCHROVEST is adding more to its bank account—this despite the fact that the price is still far below SYNCHROVEST's *Cost Per Share!*

Only on 6/71 does it finally dawn on you what SYNCHROVEST has been doing. "Tap City" at the market's bottom, SYNCHROVEST knew it could invest only $100 a month maximum—because that is all it had coming in. Doing that would freeze its advantage over Dollar Cost and maintain its comfortable lead of 51 additional shares. After all, it had already proved its worth not only in the extra shares it owned, but in its loss protection as well. Yet, every cell of its servomechanism was shouting, "Go for it! Go for it!"

There was only one way for SYNCHROVEST to "go for it," and that was by *reducing its investments and building up a bank account in anticipation of the possibility of a further price decline and greater buying opportunities, thereby increasing its lead over the Dollar Cost Averager.* A tentative stab at this is seen at our final entry when the price nodded ever so slightly and immediately received a game but necessarily mild sting from an aroused SYNCHROVEST.

The Amakudari Fund subsequently did move a little lower before moving into higher territory. Thus, it is reasonable to assume that SYNCHROVEST made a profit, or at least, no loss, particularly if bank interest is taken into account. Thousands of other investors, Dollar Cost Averagers and Hit or Missers alike, suffered severe losses in this and other stocks; and the Lump Summers who bought Amakudari at the high (who knows from the high?) and are *still* down 50% or so, will most appreciate the faithful performance of waggly-tailed SYNCHROVEST which, although it may not, in this bleak outing, have brought you back the game, at least returned your arrow to you.

"AMAKUDARI" FUND

Dollar Cost Averaging
$100 Monthly

Date	Price	Investment	Shares Bought
1/68	10.00	100	10.0
2/68	9.69	100	10.3
3/68	9.67	100	10.3
4/68	11.84	100	8.4
5/68	13.67	100	7.3
6/68	14.02	100	7.1
7/68	12.97	100	7.7
8/68	13.52	100	7.4
9/68	15.07	100	6.6
10/68	14.92	100	6.7
11/68	17.08	100	5.9
12/68	17.27	100	5.8
Dist:		99	6.7
1/69	16.15	100	6.2
2/69	14.20	100	7.0
3/69	14.90	100	6.7
4/69	15.64	100	6.4
5/69	15.73	100	6.4
6/69	13.94	100	7.2
7/69	12.25	100	8.2
8/69	13.02	100	7.7
9/69	13.46	100	7.4
10/69	14.95	100	6.7
11/69	14.21	100	7.0
12/69	13.97	100	7.2

Chart E

"AMAKUDARI" FUND

Dollar Cost Averaging
$100 Monthly

Date	Price	Investment	Shares Bought
1/70	12.64	100	7.9
2/70	12.41	100	8.1
3/70	12.02	100	8.3
4/70	8.51	100	11.8
5/70	6.32	100	15.8
6/70	5.46	100	18.3
7/70	5.35	100	18.7
8/70	5.57	100	18.0
9/70	6.48	100	15.4
10/70	6.25	100	16.0
11/70	6.34	100	15.8
12/70	6.69	100	14.9
1/71	7.29	100	13.7
2/71	7.33	100	13.6
3/71	7.97	100	12.5
4/71	8.01	100	12.5
5/71	7.58	100	13.2
6/71	7.30	100	13.7

Chart E (cont'd.)

Chart E-1

"AMAKUDARI" FUND

SYNCHROVEST

Date	Price	Investment	Shares Bought	Shares Owned	Total Investment	Cost Per Share	Credit Balance
1/68	10.00	$100	10.0	10.0	100	10	0
2/68	9.69	75	7.7	17.7	175	10	25
3/68	9.67	75	7.8	25.5	250	10	50
4/68	11.84	62	5.2	30.7	312	10	88
5/68	13.67	53	3.9	34.6	365	10	135
6/68	14.02	53	3.8	38.4	418	11	182
7/68	12.97	64	4.9	43.3	482	11	218
8/68	13.52	59	4.4	47.7	541	11	259
9/68	15.07	55	3.6	51.3	596	12	304
10/68	14.92	60	4.0	55.3	656	12	344
11/68	17.08	53	3.1	58.4	709	12	391
12/68	17.27	53	3.1	61.5	762		438
Dist:		66	4.5	66.0	828	13	438
1/69	16.15	61	3.8	69.8	889	13	477
2/69	14.20	70	4.9	74.7	959	13	507
3/69	14.90	65	4.4	79.1	1,024	13	542
4/69	15.64	61	3.9	83.0	1,085	13	581
5/69	15.73	61	3.9	86.9	1,146	13	620
6/69	13.94	70	5.0	91.9	1,216	13	650
7/69	12.25	81 + 52 = 133	10.9	102.8	1,349	13	617
8/69	13.02	75	5.8	108.6	1,424	13	642
9/69	13.46	75	5.6	114.2	1,499	13	667
10/69	14.95	65	4.3	118.5	1,564	13	702
11/69	14.21	70	4.9	123.4	1,634	13	732
12/69	13.97	70	5.0	128.4	1,704	13	762

1/70	12.64	75	5.9	134.3	1,779	13	787
2/70	12.41	81 + 63 = 144	11.6	145.9	1,923	13	743
*3/70	12.02	81 + 59 = 140	11.6	157.5	2,063	13	703
4/70	8.51	108 + 309 = 417	49.0	206.5	2,480	12	386
5/70	6.32	150 + 193 = 343	54.3	260.8	2,823	11	143
6/70	5.46	165 + 72 = 237	43.4	304.2	3,060	10	6
7/70	5.35	106	19.8	324.0	3,166	10	0
8/70	5.57	100	18.0	342.0	3,266	10	0
9/70	6.48	100	15.4	357.4	3,366	9	0
10/70	6.25	100	16.0	373.4	3,466	9	0
11/70	6.34	100	15.8	389.2	3,566	9	0
12/70	6.69	97	14.5	403.7	3,663	9	3
1/71	7.29	97 + 1 = 98	13.4	417.1	3,761	9	5
2/71	7.33	97 + 1 = 98	13.4	430.5	3,859	9	7
3/71	7.97	85 + 1 = 86	10.8	441.3	3,945	9	21
4/71	8.01	85 + 3 = 88	11.0	452.3	4,033	9	33
5/71	7.58	85 + 4 = 89	11.7	464.0	4,122	9	44
6/71	7.30	97 + 13 = 110	15.1	479.1	4,232		34

FINAL RESULTS

SYNCHROVEST

Investment: $4,232
Loss: $735 (minus bank interest)
Shares Owned: 479
Profit when price returns to original $10.00: $558 (13%) + bank interest

Dollar Cost Averaging

Investment: $4,299
Loss: $1,138
Shares Owned: 433
Profit when price returns to original $10.00: $31 (less than 1%).

*Observe the speed with which SYNCHROVEST reduces the investor's Cost Per Share from this point on.

The famous Dollar Cost Averaging chart below appeared, in more detailed form, in Johnson's Investment Company Charts, 1958 edition, to illustrate the superiority of Dollar Cost Averaging over Lump-Sum Investing. *Note that SYNCHROVEST led Dollar Cost Averaging every step of the way.*

Bank interest has not been added to SYNCHROVEST's credit balance.

DOLLAR COST AVERAGING

Price	Investment	Shares Bought	Total Shares	Profit (Loss)
$10	$100	10.0	10.0	—
$ 8	$100	12.5	22.5	($20.00)
$ 5	$100	20.0	42.5	($87.50)
$ 4	$100	25.0	67.5	(130.00)
$ 5	$100	20.0	87.5	($67.50)
$ 8	$100	12.5	100.0	200.00
$10	$100	10.0	110.0	400.00
$ 8	$100	12.5	122.5	180.00
$ 5	$100	20.0	142.5	(187.50)
$ 4	$100	25.0	167.5	(330.00)
$ 5	$100	20.0	187.5	(167.50)
$ 8	$100	12.5	200.0	400.00

TOTAL INVESTMENT: $1,200

PROFIT: $400.00

% PROFIT: 33%

Chart F

SYNCHROVEST

Investment	Shares Bought	Total Shares	Total Investment	CPS	Credit BALANCE	Profit (Loss)
$ 75	7.5	7.5	$ 75	10	$ 25	—
$100	12.5	20.0	$ 175	9	$ 25	($ 15.00)
$125	25.0	45.0	$ 300	7	0	($ 75.00)
$100	25.0	70.0	$ 400	6	0	($120.00)
$ 90	18.0	88.0	$ 490	6	$ 10	($ 50.00)
$ 56	7.0	95.0	$ 546	6	$ 54	$214.00
$ 60	6.0	101.0	$ 606	6	$ 94	$404.00
$ 75	9.4	110.4	$ 681	6	$119	$202.20
$144	28.8	139.2	$ 825	6	$ 75	($129.00)
$175	43.8	183.0	$1000	5	0	($268.00)
$100	20.0	203.0	$1100	5	0	($ 85.00)
$ 63	7.9	210.9	$1163	6	$ 37	$524.20

TOTAL INVESTMENT: $1,163.00

PROFIT: $524.00
(31% more than Dollar Cost Averager)

% PROFIT: 45%

Chart F (cont'd.)

% PROFIT (LOSS)

Price	Lump Sum Investor	Dollar Cost Averager	SYNCHROVESTOR
10	—	—	—
8	(20%)	(10%)	(9%)
5	(50%)	(29%)	(25%)
4	(60%)	(33%)	(30%)
5	(50%)	(14%)	(10%)
8	(20%)	33%	39%
10	—	57%	67%
8	(20%)	23%	30%
5	(50%)	(21%)	(16%)*
4	(60%)	(33%)	(27%)
5	(50%)	(15%)	(8%)
8	(20%)	33%	45%

*All losses are expressed as a percentage of money invested, but since SYNCHROVEST often has less invested than Dollar Cost Averaging, its *dollar loss* tends to be sharply less than would be suggested by comparative percentage figures. Here, for example, SYNCHROVEST has a loss of only $129.00 while Dollar Cost Averaging's loss is $187.50—45% greater than SYNCHROVEST's!

Chart F-1

Let's take another look at that fascinating chart and assume that these are monthly prices of the stock and that the period covers 12 months. A benighted investor who plunked down his entire $1,200 in a lump sum in January and paid $10 a share never, at any time during the year, showed a profit on his investment. And if the stock behaved in an identical fashion the following year, the lump summer would still not see a profit. Nor would he make a penny's worth of capital gains in the stock if it repeated that performance every year for a hundred years. He's locked into a mathematical cul-de-sac.

The *Dollar Cost Averager* displays a far more balanced attack. At the end of the first year, he has scored an impressive 33% gain. And at the end of the second year—assuming an identical performance of the stock—the *Dollar Cost Averager* would show a profit for the two-year period of . . . 33%. If he persists with his program for a hundred years he will *never*, at any year's end, have a profit of more than 33% on his entire investment. The *Dollar Cost Averager*, too, is locked into a mathematical cul-de-sac. Granted, the food is better and his linen is changed daily, but he is still not much better off than the stock freaks in Joseph Farris's marvelous cartoon who find themselves in hell guarded by grinning, pitchfork-wielding devils. It is a familiar kind of hell—the boardroom of a brokerage house—complete with ticker tape and quotron summary. And one fellow turns to the other fellow and says, "You mean all we can do is watch? We can't buy or sell?"

The SYNCHROVESTOR's experience with the chart is quite different. Like the long-distance runner, his heartbeat, at rest, is much slower than that of other people. It *has* to be, so that when the time comes for a burst of blazing speed, he will have the reserve to accomodate him. If you *start* a race with a normal heartbeat, you'll soon reach your maximum and fall by the wayside. For that reason, the SYNCHROVESTOR's heart, at rest, beats at a slower rate. So long as he stays even with the market, he invests only 75% of his normal potential. The *Dollar Cost Averager*'s heart, on the other hand, always beats at 100% of capacity, leaving him no reserve at all.

In the first year, SYNCHROVEST chalked up a 45% profit, soundly defeating the *Dollar Cost Averager.* But, unlike Dollar Cost, SYNCHROVEST won't be trapped. Year after year, it *increases* its profit percentage and extends its lead over the static *Dollar Cost Averager.*

At the end of four years—*and even without taking into account the bank interest the* SYNCHROVESTOR *would have earned on his Credit Balance, the extra shares it would have purchased, and the greater profit afforded by these shares*—the SYNCHROVEST account would show a profit of 50%! This is a 50% profit on every dollar invested—including the last dollar invested on the last month of the last year.

SYNCHROVEST—SECOND YEAR

Price	Investment	Shares Purchased	Total Shares	Total Investment	Cost Per Share	Credit Balance
10	60	6.0	216.9	1223	6	77
8	75	9.4	226.3	1298	6	102
5	140	28.0	254.3	1438	6	62
4	162	40.5	294.8	1600	5	0
5	100	20.0	314.8	1700	5	0
8	63	7.9	322.7	1763	5	37
10	50	5.0	327.7	1813	6	87
8	75	9.4	337.1	1888	6	112
5	142	28.4	365.5	2030	6	70
4	170	42.5	408.0	2200	5	0
5	100	20.0	428.0	2300	5	0
8	63	7.9	435.9	2363	5	37

SYNCHROVEST—THIRD YEAR

Price	Investment	Shares Purchased	Total Shares	Total Investment	Cost Per Share	Credit Balance
10	50	5.0	440.9	2413	5	87
8	63	7.9	448.8	2476	6	124
5	145	29.0	477.8	2621	5	79
4	145	36.3	514.1	2766	5	34
5	100	20.0	534.1	2866	5	34
8	63	7.9	542.0	2929	5	71
10	50	5.0	547.0	2979	5	121
8	63	7.9	554.9	3042	5	158
5	100	20.0	574.9	3142	5	158
4	165	41.3	616.2	3307	5	93
5	100	20.0	636.2	3407	5	93
8	63	7.9	644.1	3470	5	130

SYNCHROVEST—FOURTH YEAR

Price	Investment	Shares Purchased	Total Shares	Total Investment	Cost Per Share	Credit Balance
10	50	5.0	649.1	3520	5	180
8	63	7.9	657.0	3583	5	217
5	100	20.0	677.0	3683	5	217
4	179	44.8	721.8	3862	5	138
5	100	20.0	741.8	3962	5	138
8	63	7.9	749.7	4025	5	175
10	50	5.0	754.7	4075	5	225
8	63	7.9	762.6	4138	5	262
5	100	20.0	782.6	4238	5	262
4	191	47.8	830.4	4429	5	171
5	100	20.0	850.4	4529	5	171
8	63	7.9	858.3	4592	5	208

SUMMARY

SYNCHROVEST	DOLLAR COST AVERAGER
1st Year—Profit: $ 524 (45%)	Profit: $ 400 (33%)
2nd Year—Profit: $1124 (48%)	Profit: $ 800 (33%)
3rd Year—Profit: $1683 (49%)	Profit: $1200 (33%)
4th Year—Profit: $2274 (50%)	Profit: $1600 (33%)
Total shares: 858.3	Total shares: 800
Bank Account: $208 + interest	Bank Account: 0

It would be easy, of course, to construct a chart for SYNCHROVEST so fabulous as to plague the reader with seizures while he waited impatiently for the market to open. And it would be as fair a paradigm as any other, for who can say a particular stock—or hundreds of them, for that matter—have not behaved in exactly that fashion sometime in history? We might, for example, begin our chart in a period of dullness and hold the price of the stock in a narrow trading range for a period of months and even years, allowing SYNCHROVEST to build up substantial reserves. Then we would simply let the bottom fall out of the stock and allow SYNCHROVEST's massive reserves to move in for the kill at the lows. The *Dollar Cost Averager*, having committed enormous sums of capital to the stock at much higher prices, would be wrecked.

But it is not our intention to stack the deck. SYNCHROVEST does not need that kind of puffery. But to further illustrate the principles behind its operation, let us use the same chart as before, only this time, instead of beginning the chart at the high, $10, let us start at the first low, $4, and, with that single manipulation done with, adhere faithfully to the remaining secular prices.

Where the original chart began at $10 and ended two points down at $8, it now happens that we have begun at $4 and ended one point higher, at $5 a share. Yet, even though we are now closing the year at a *higher* price, the *Dollar Cost Averager* will find something quite unexpected and unpleasant in his Christmas stocking: a 17% loss! $200!

Worse, if the stock behaves the same way the following year and the *Dollar Cost Averager* resolutely invests his $100 a month, he will exit December with the identical loss—17%! And, since he now has twice as much invested, his dollar loss will be doubled! After a hundred Decembers of this, his loss will *remain* frozen at 17%. If we are still using dollars then, the loss would amount to $20,000!

Try that same stunt with SYNCHROVEST and it will conclude your first year with a loss of only 7%—$70—and a bank account (excluding interest) of $140. Feed it the same stock prices next year and SYNCHROVEST will soon figure out what you're doing and the kind of game you're playing with it. Quickly determining that the price of $4 is the low of the year, SYNCHROVEST will go to work on that price only, hitting it with stiffer jabs every time it comes around. By the end of the second year, SYNCHROVEST has not only reduced its loss to 6% and increased its *Credit Balance,* but has accumulated more shares than *Dollar Cost Averager*!

SYNCHROVEST—FIRST YEAR

Price	Investment	Shares Purchased	Total Shares	Total Investment	Cost Per Share	Credit Balance
4	75	18.8	18.8	75	4	25
5	60	12.0	30.8	135	4	65
8	50	6.3	37.1	185	5	115
10	50	5.0	42.1	235	6	165
8	75	9.4	51.5	310	6	190
5	158	31.6	83.1	468	6	132
4	216	54.0	137.1	684	5	16
5	100	20.0	157.1	784	5	16
8	63	7.9	165.0	847	5	53
10	50	5.0	170.0	897	5	103
8	63	7.9	177.9	960	5	140
5	100	20.0	197.9	1060	5	140

SYNCHROVEST—SECOND YEAR

Price	Investment	Shares Purchased	Total Shares	Total Investment	Cost Per Share	Credit Balance
4	160	40.0	237.9	1220	5	80
5	100	20.0	257.9	1320	5	80
8	63	7.9	265.8	1383	5	117
10	50	5.0	270.8	1433	5	167
8	63	7.9	278.7	1496	5	204
5	100	20.0	298.7	1596	5	204
4	176	44.0	342.7	1772	5	128
5	100	20.0	362.7	1872	5	128
8	63	7.9	370.6	1935	5	165
10	50	5.0	375.6	1985	5	215
8	63	7.9	383.5	2048	5	252
5	100	20.0	403.5	2148	5	252

SYNCHROVEST—THIRD YEAR

Price	Investment	Shares Purchased	Total Shares	Total Investment	Cost Per Share	Credit Balance
4	188	47.0	450.5	2336	5	164
5	100	20.0	470.5	2436	5	164
8	63	7.9	478.4	2499	5	201
10	50	5.0	483.4	2549	5	251
8	63	7.9	491.3	2612	5	288
5	100	20.0	511.3	2712	5	288
4	197	49.3	560.6	2909	5	191
5	100	20.0	580.6	3009	5	191
8	63	7.9	588.5	3072	5	228
10	50	5.0	593.5	3122	5	278
8	63	7.9	601.4	3185	5	315
5	100	20.0	621.4	3285	5	315

SYNCHROVEST—FOURTH YEAR

Price	Investment	Shares Purchased	Total Shares	Total Investment	Cost Per Share	Credit Balance
4	204	51.0	672.4	3489	5	211
5	100	20.0	692.4	3589	5	211
8	63	7.9	700.3	3652	5	248
10	50	5.0	705.3	3702	5	298
8	63	7.9	713.2	3765	5	335
5	100	20.0	733.2	3865	5	335
4	209	52.3	785.5	4074	5	226
5	100	20.0	805.5	4174	5	226
8	63	7.9	813.4	4237	5	263
10	50	5.0	818.4	4287	5	313
8	63	7.9	826.3	4350	5	350
5	100	20.0	846.3	4450	5	350

SUMMARY

SYNCHROVEST				DOLLAR COST AVERAGER		
1st	Year—Loss:	$ 70	(6.6%)	Loss:	$200	(16.7%)
2nd	Year—Loss:	$130	(6.1%)	Loss:	$400	(16.7%)
3rd	Year—Loss:	$178	(5.4%)	Loss:	$600	(16.7%)
4th	Year—Loss:	$218	(4.9%)	Loss:	$800	(16.7%)
Total shares: 846.3				Total shares: 800		
Bank Account: $350 + interest				Bank Account: 0		

SYNCHROVEST will continue to reduce its percentage loss and increase its share lead over *Dollar Cost Averager.* Presented with the almost impossible task of producing a profit at $5 a share while continuing to purchase shares at $10 and $8, SYNCHROVEST will do exactly that! Indeed, after only four years, it has reduced its loss to less than 5%. *If we had allowed bank interest to accumulate on our Credit Balance, the extra muscle would have potentiated* SYNCHROVEST*'s punches at the $4 prices, increased its bank account, and quite possibly propelled it into the win column even in the fourth December!*

Obviously, with a *Cost Per Share* of $5 (rounded), SYNCHROVEST already enjoys a profit—and a fine one—on those months in which the stock price is $8 or $10; but our concern here is with year-end prices.

Even if SYNCHROVEST *stopped* investing, the relentless interest on his *Credit Balance* would eventually bail him out and drag him, kicking and screaming, to a victorious New Year's Eve celebration in the not too distant future.

The *Dollar Cost Averager* could stop too, but it would never affect his 16.7% loss one way or the other. Every December it would clatter into his bedroom, the ghost of Christmas past, level a bony finger at him, and chuckle, "*Now*, do you believe?"

A stock market crash is catnip to SYNCHROVEST. The moaning and lamentation of fairweather gunslingers are music to its ears. While the Lump Summer and the *Dollar Cost Averager* watch in horror as their profits slip away, the SYNCHROVESTOR, knowing he is merely exchanging a small immediate profit for a greater eventual profit will be rooting *against* the market, hoping against hope that his stock will be driven down to its triggering point.

It's a great feeling!

The foregoing tests with the Johnson's Investment Company Chart were made with one overriding purpose in mind: to reveal the interior workings of SYNCHROVEST and to familiarize the reader with its basic principles. Toward that end, we have deliberately suppressed a critical feature of our rather remarkable instrument, and reserved it, so to speak, for the postgraduate course.

We have learned that when we divide the price of the stock into our *Cost Per Share*, multiply that figure by our *Base Investment*, and derive a sum that is half or less of our *Planned Investment*, it is time to "shift gears"—to discard our *Base Investment* and go on to bigger things. The *Base Investment* has served its purpose: it has protected us during our first faltering steps and guided us to a profit of 50% or more on our money. If we had begun our program using our full *Planned Investment* instead, and the market had immediately gone into a tailspin, we would be—as the saying goes—up the creek without a paddle. SYNCHROVEST would continue to demand from us the maximum investment each month—the same amount that our friend, the Dollar Cost Averager, is investing—and at the bottom we would both be scrounging around for cigar butts in the same park.

By buying fewer shares at the top and a greater number on the way down, the *Base Investment* not only enables us to outperform the Dollar Cost Averager even when we have no cash reserve in the bank, but it goes to work immediately to build up a cash reserve. Like a lineman in his three-point stance tensed for the final "hut", the Dollar Cost Averager has hurled himself forward—into thin air. The market has simply stepped aside and allowed him to somersault into the Astro-turf. In jujitsu, this breaking of your opponent's balance is called *kuzushi.* SYNCHROVEST defends against it by not concentrating all its power on one leg.

But now that we have our 50% profit and reserves in the bank, we are sitting on a comfortable lead and can proceed to run up the score. The switch to our *Planned Investment* enables us to do this.

The time will come, God willing, when you will divide the price of your stock into your *Cost Per Share*, multiply by your *Planned Investment*, and come up with a figure that is 50% or less of your *Planned Investment.* The first time this happened to you, you were using your *Base Investment* as a multiplier; and it was a signal that you had made a 50% profit and should immediately switch to using your *Planned Investment* as a multiplier. To keep straight in your mind which multiplier is currently being used, begin your program by noting both of them somewhere at the top of your chart:

<u>Base Investment $75</u>

Planned Investment $100

The *Base Investment* is underlined to avoid confusion. When the time comes to "shift gears," strike out the *Base Investment* like so:

~~<u>Base Investment $75</u>~~

Planned Investment $100

But now, as we said, you are using the *Planned Investment* and SYNCHROVEST *again* has called for an investment that is 50% or less of your *Planned Investment.* What this means is simply that you have doubled your money. You have a 100% profit on every dollar invested, plus who knows how much bank interest on your cash reserves.

Now, if you have a 100% profit in the market, SYNCHROVEST believes you are better out than in. Would you doubt an investment adviser that has told you exactly when to buy, exactly how much to buy, and doubled your money for you?

If you have doubled your money, the market is much more likely to be nearer its high and your profits are exposed to an ever-growing risk. The market could, of course, go higher; and may indeed go much higher. But in the end, SYNCHROVEST believes the trade-off is much more advantageous to you. Because no matter how much higher it does go, it *must* turn down sooner or later—and SYNCHROVEST, racing after it with its largest army in history, will meet it head on. The army is made up of your *Credit Balance* plus the proceeds of the sale of all your shares.

Thus, when you have doubled your money, sell out and add the proceeds to your bank *Credit Balance*—and then immediately begin a new SYNCHROVEST program. Continue to use your *Planned Investment*; you will never again need to bother with your *Base Investment.* In actual practice, it may prove more convenient to maintain sufficient shares in your account amounting to one month's investment. In other words, if your *Planned Investment* is $100 a month, sell all your shares except $100 worth—and count that as your first purchase of the new program. Your new *Cost Per Share,* then, will be exactly the price the stock is selling for at that moment. Note that subsequent purchases will have an intensified effect on this *Cost Per Share,* as it is far easier for a single purchase to affect the *Cost Per Share* of a lean portfolio than a more massive one. Which is exactly what we meant when we described SYNCHROVEST as racing after a climbing market.

Probably the most astonishing of SYNCHROVEST's achievements is the manner in which it maximizes the use of its reserves here at the market top. It may seem that after selling off all its shares, SYNCHROVEST would need a decline equal to the market's rise in order to manage to buy back all the shares it had sold; but this would be to ignore a fascinating contrariety: SYNCHROVEST's *Credit Balance* is now swollen with the proceeds of the stock sale, and the slightest triggering of this fund unleashes a torrent of capital that can reach awesome proportions. At no time is this process more stunning than during a market decline immediately following a SYNCHROVEST sale. If SYNCHROVEST has sold out at $10 a share, and the price of the stock is now $9, SYNCHROVEST is using the market's own money—pure profit—to aid in its clean-up campaign. And even though it may have taken years to accumulate the shares in the first place, SYNCHROVEST could buy them back (and more) in months—even though the market never fully retreats to its original position. This re-cycling process keeps your portfolio constantly fresh and green—and the reservoir or your *Credit Balance* bubbling with healthful activity.

The material that follows may excite our readers to such an extent that perhaps a medical check-up may be in order for those not too sanguine about their physical condition. What we are going to do is run the Johnson's Investment Company Chart once again—and *this* time allow SYNCHROVEST to sell when it is supposed to, when it has doubled your money. Although the results may or may not be indicative of what you can accomplish in your investment program, they do demonstrate SYNCHROVEST's incredible potential—now cautious and conservative as though seeking to preserve the safety of a widow's mite, now chasing and striking with the ferocity of Australia's deadly taipan snake.

SYNCHROVEST—YEAR II

(First year remains the same as before. Switch from Base Investment to Planned Investment was made in July of that year.)

Price	Investment	Shares Purchased	Total Shares	Total Investment	Cost Per Share	Credit Balance
10	60	6.0	216.9	1,223	6	77
8	75	9.4	226.3	1,298	6	102
5	140	28.0	254.3	1,438	6	62
4	162	40.5	294.8	1,600	5	0
5	100	20.0	314.8	1,700	5	0
8	63	7.9	322.7	1,763	5	37
10	(Sold 322.7 shares at $3,227)					3,264
	100	10.0	10.0	100	10	3,264
8	941	117.6	127.6	1,041	8	2,423
5	1,372	274.4	402.0	2,413	6	1,151
4	726	181.5	583.5	3,139	5	525
5	100	20.0	603.5	3,239	5	525
8	63	7.9	611.4	3,302	5	562

~~Base Investment $75~~

Planned Investment $100

SHARES WORTH:	$4,891
CREDIT BALANCE:	562
TOTAL:	$5,453
INVESTMENT:	$2,400
PROFIT:	$3,053
% PROFIT:	127.2%

SYNCHROVEST—YEAR III

Price	Investment	Shares Purchased	Total Shares	Total Investment	Cost Per Share	Credit Balance
10	(Sold 611.4 shares at $6,114)					6,676
	100	10.0	10.0	100	10	6,676
8	1,794	224.3	234.3	1,894	8	4,982
5	2,651	530.2	764.5	4,545	6	2,431
4	1,366	341.5	1,106.0	5,911	5	1,165
5	100	20.0	1,126.0	6,011	5	1,165
8	63	7.9	1,133.9	6,074	5	1,202
10	(Sold 1,133.9 shares at $11,339)					12,541
	100	10.0	10.0	100	10	12,541
8	3,260	407.5	417.5	3,360	8	9,381
5	4,851	970.2	1,387.7	8,211	6	4,630
4	2,465	616.3	2,004.0	10,676	5	2,265
5	100	20.0	2,024.0	10,776	5	2,265
8	63	7.9	2,031.9	10,839	5	2,302

SHARES WORTH:	$16,255
CREDIT BALANCE:	2,302
TOTAL:	$18,557
INVESTMENT:	3,600
PROFIT:	$14,957
% PROFIT:	415.5%

SYNCHROVEST—YEAR IV

Price	Investment	Shares Purchased	Total Shares	Total Investment	Cost Per Share	Credit Balance
10	(Sold 2,031.9 shares at $20,319)					22,621
	100	10.0	10.0	100	10	22,621
8	5,780	722.5	732.5	5,880	8	16,941
5	8,631	1,726.2	2,458.7	14,511	6	8,410
4	4,355	1,088.8	3,547.5	18,866	5	4,155
5	100	20.0	3,567.5	18,966	5	4,155
8	63	7.9	3,575.4	19,029	5	4,192
10	(Sold 3,575.4 shares at $35,754)					39,946
	100	10.0	10.0	100	10	39,946
8	10,112	1,264.0	1,274.0	10,212	8	29,934
5	15,127	3,025.4	4,299.4	25,339	6	14,907
4	7,604	1,901.0	6,200.4	32,943	5	7,403
5	100	20.0	6,220.4	33,043	5	7,403
8	63	7.9	6,228.3	33,106	5	7,440

DOLLAR COST AVERAGER'S RESULTS

TOTAL VALUE:	$6,400
INVESTMENT:	4,800
PROFIT:	$1,600

% PROFIT: 33.3%
NUMBER OF SHARES: 800

SYNCHROVEST'S RESULTS

SHARES WORTH:	$49,826
CREDIT BALANCE:	7,440
TOTAL:	$57,266
INVESTMENT:	4,800
PROFIT:	$52,466

% PROFIT: 1,093%
NUMBER OF SHARES: 6,228.3

Note that these staggering results were obtained in a stock that never rose a single penny above its original price—and indeed closed 20% lower! Note also that the final profit of $52,466 does not include the substantial bank interest that would have been earned on your eye-popping *Credit Balance,* nor the extra shares it could have purchased at opportune times. This interest alone probably surpasses Dollar Cost Averager's entire profit. *And remember that all this was achieved with an investment of only $100 a month for four years!*

In our first experiment, we also tampered with the Johnson's Investment Company Chart a bit to see what would have happened had we begun investing at the low instead of the high. In our reconstruction, the stock opened the year at $4 a share and closed the year at $5 a share. Here again, to make a point, we suppressed the critical feature of SYNCHROVEST that enables it to unleash all its power. Now let us take our finger off the "Suppress Button" and see what would have happened if SYNCHROVEST had been permitted to sell out every time it made a 100% profit:

FINAL RESULTS AFTER 4 YEARS

SYNCHROVEST	DOLLAR COST AVERAGER
Profit: $25,021 (+521.3%)	LOSS: ($800) (-16.7%)
Total Shares: 3,527.5	Total Shares: 800
Bank Account: $12,183 plus interest	Bank Account: 0

The Special Bank Account That Could Outperform Your Stock 6

Everybody feels sorry for those poor Manhattan Indians who were conned by Peter Minuit of the Dutch West India Company into parting with Manhattan Island for a mere $24 in trinkets and beads back in 1626. Few people know, however, that it was not $24 in trinkets and beads, but 60 guilders—and 60 guilders was equivalent to $39.00. Which is more like it! Fewer people know that the Indian Chief who handed over the keys, Conquelquelpo'po'dipatrimonio, immediately deposited the funds in the Dutch Trading Post Savings and Loan Co., in a trust account for the benefit of his descendants at a guaranteed annual rate of 6%—the same rate available to depositors today. The English seized the bank when they took over in 1664, renamed it The First Corn and Acorn Squash Bank and Trust Co., but maintained its current accounts while continuing the bank's policy of paying the highest dividend rates allowed by law. When the Dutch regained control for a brief period, they could not understand why their promotional mailings to their Indian depositors urging them to continue their savings program came back stamped UNKNOWN AT THIS ADDRESS—until a vice president remembered that the Dutch themselves had killed almost all the Indians between 1640 and 1645. Before they had a chance to seize all the accounts of their deceased depositors, the Dutch were driven out by the English again and fled to Holland. They were immediately imprisoned for unlawful flight, and the holding company that controlled the bank, Mededogen, Ltd., took over the management and continued to service its accounts by mail, postage-paid. Last May, a new director was appointed. His first task was a complete computerization of the bank's records. What he found in one dusty book nearly gave him apoplexy.

"Strijd en onbillijkheden ruimen het veld voor het levend bewijs van Liefde's bestuur!" he gasped. "And fast, you numbskull!"

"As close as I can come to it in American dollars, sir," a clerk named Leroy responded, "$39 deposited in 1626 at 6% interest would now be worth $20 billion, sir."

A guilder sticking to his sleeve, the new director moaned, "Leroyyy, find out what the assessed valuation of Manhattan is now, you incompetent, soon-to-be-fired wretch!"

"The last time I looked, sir, it was $15 billion, land included."

"Als iedereen zou weten . . ." the director groaned in despair. Suddenly he brightened. "Why, of course! *Van nederlaag tot overwinning!* I think we're safe. I can't imagine anyone still living who carries such a name. Imagine—" he laughed, "Conquelquelpo'po'dipatrimonio!"

The clerk looked up in surprise. "Why, that's my mother's maiden name, sir!"

The moral of this tale is: Never underestimate a savings account. In the past few years, unreasoning fears of inflation and the growing financial sophistication of the public concerning equity investments have painted the savings account as a haven for the pennies of rubes. The virtual collapse of the stock market in 1970 and its failure to recover lost ground despite the showboating of the 30 Dow Jones Industrials, forced many to the bitter conclusion that stocks aren't the great hedge against inflation they were touted to be in the preceding boom years. And billions of disenchanted dollars poured into banks.

As for inflation, is it really the ogre it is made out to be? Between 1958 and 1965, consumer prices rose only 1.3 percent a year on average; and in about half of the past 25 years they increased no more than 1 or 2 percent. Many items, such as refrigerators, appliances, radios, television sets, plane fares, are cheaper today than they were decades ago; and the items that have soared in price, with very few exceptions, have not outrun the purchasing power of the dollar in a savings account! Even a man's haircut—often used as a prime example of the inflationary spiral—can be purchased today at its 1941 price of 52 cents, provided that 52 cents was deposited in a savings account in 1941 at 5% interest.

The Consumer Price Index does *not* measure the cost of living, but the cost of keeping up with the Joneses. The 400-odd items that make up this index have been frequently changed over the years; old basic food staples such as lard, oats, and soda crackers have been replaced by items our parents might have considered luxuries, i.e., steak, frozen shrimp, chocolate syrup, and layer cake! So don't be unduly alarmed by a climbing Price Index.

The savings account that SYNCHROVEST builds up for you cannot, by any stretch of the imagination, be viewed as idle money. Indeed, presented with a dull security that fluctuates sluggishly over a period of years, SYNCHROVEST may build up a bank account of such heft that the relentless compound interest alone will defeat the fully-invested Dollar Cost Averager year after year.

Your savings account is an integral part of your SYNCHROVEST program, and many times—particularly in today's nervous market—it can be the happiest part.

The best type of bank account in which to maintain your *Credit Balance* is the "day-of-deposit-to-day-of-withdrawal" account offered by savings banks. Here you will get 5¼% on your money (5.47% actually, thanks to continuous compounding), and interest is paid on every dollar in your account for every day that it stays there. In other types of accounts, you will not receive interest on money that is withdrawn before the end of the quarter. To observe how the "day-of-deposit-to-day-of-withdrawal" account works to your advantage with SYNCHROVEST, imagine that SYNCHROVEST has directed you to invest $1,000 from your *Credit Balance* account on December 1st. When you withdraw that $1,000 from the bank, you would ordinarily lose two months interest on it—interest for October and November amounting to some $9.00—because banks normally give you interest only on money remaining until the end of the quarter (in this case, December 31st). With the "day-of-deposit-to-day-of-withdrawal" account, however, the bank will credit your account with interest earned for October and November, and will pay it to you at the end of the quarter provided you maintain a minimum balance in your account—generally $1.00. Therefore, we will use the "day-of-deposit-to-day-of-withdrawal" account with our SYNCHROVEST program, and we will always keep at least a dollar in it to maintain our account and to insure that we will be paid interest for every dollar for every day it stays there.

But, since SYNCHROVEST offers us superpower investing, the perfect mate would be a super savings account—and that is exactly what West Side Federal Savings, 1790 Broadway, New York, New York, has provided us with. They call it the Pace Setter Savings Account, and it combines the best features of the "day-of-deposit-to-day-of-withdrawal" account and the regular savings account. In the Pace Setter Account, interest is paid at the rate of 5¼% (an effective yield of 5.47%) for every day your money is on deposit regardless of when you withdraw it, *and* any deposits received by the 10th of *any* month earn interest from the 1st of that month if they remain to the end of the quarter. Therefore, by selecting the 10th of the month for his stock purchase and *Credit Balance* deposits, the Synchrovestor can oomph-asize not only his bank profits, but his stock purchases as well, when his mechanism is triggered on the downside. Since he receives a full month's interest for money on deposit only 20 days, a 50% advantage, his money has actually earned at the rate of nearly 8¼% per year!

Obviously, a deposit made on the 10th will perform as indicated *for that month*, and deposits on the 10th of any month will do likewise; in subsequent months, however, these moneys will draw interest at the regular rate of 5.47%. An occasional withdrawal, too, before the end of a quarter may cancel out the *bonus* interest (not the regular interest) on part or all of any particular deposit; but it appears safe to assume that the Synchrovestor's *Credit Balance* in a Pace Setter Account will earn interest somewhere near 6%. And, at 6% interest, money doubles every 12 years!

Thus, even if SYNCHROVEST *never* triggers your *Credit Balance,* it is there piling up ever-greater profits for you every quarter, *without fail*; and you may find to your delight that, in a period in which the stock market is going nowhere at all, you are pulling farther and farther ahead of Dollar Cost Averaging through the power of your *Credit Balance* alone!

Unlike other investment systems, even when SYNCHROVEST doesn't work, it works!

The Only Kind of Stock to Buy 7

The Zen *mondo* might go something like this:

Pupil: "Wouldn't I do better by picking out a good growth stock or Mutual Fund and investing a lump sum of money in it and just forget about it?"
Master: "Have a cup of tea."

If this doesn't make sense to you, you're still trying to communicate verbally and rationally—and this just won't wash in a Zen monastery or on Wall Street. The Zen master might clout you with his staff to show you the error of your ways, but the stock market will break it over your head and charge you for the breakage. Rudolph L. Weissman, a vice president for research over at W.E. Hutton & Co., had a little fun recently with a non-Zen lesson for investors who think they can pick growth stocks on the basis of past performance. He compiled a list of ten highly-touted growth stocks that bubbled merrily in the 1950's and gave every indication of percolating through their lids in the soaring sixties. A lot of sophisticated investors put a lump sum of money into some of them back then. Maybe you did too.

Here's what happened after nine years in a generally up market:

COMPANY	Price 12/31/60	Price 12/31/69
Aluminum Co. of America	108	71
American Cyanamid	30	26
American Tel	54	49
Corn Products (CPC Int.)	43	32
Ford	46	41
General Electric	100	78
International Paper	42	37
Owens-Illinois	58	62
Parke Davis	51	35
Scott Paper	31	34

I'd like to add some prices of my own, the prices at which those same stocks were selling only five months later, on May 26, 1970:

Aluminum Co. of America	50
American Cyanamid	22
American Tel	43
Corn Products (CPS Int.)	28
Ford	40
General Electric	60
International Paper	28
Owens-Illinois	39
Parke Davis	16
Scott Paper	26

Awful, isn't it? Well, then, you say, what about trying to pick mini-growth stocks of the future—little known companies like "Fink Finance" just getting started—and hop on board before the public gets wise?

In order for any investment program to work, the price of the stock should be higher toward the end than at the beginning—although, as has been shown, SYNCHROVEST has the unique potential of wringing profits out of the most modest advances from the bottom of the market. If you lump-sum with a "Fink Finance," you are almost certain to lose; and if you use SYNCHROVEST on it, you might follow it all the way down to zero, just as you would with Dollar Cost

Averaging, and there you are. It is safer, therefore, to select stocks of large established companies, or Mutual Funds whose managements have proved in the crash of '70 that they can "take it" and come back. *What we look for in a security now is no longer high-voltage growth, but merely some reasonable assurance that, regardless of changing fortunes, it will come back.* The list we have just given you undoubtedly would have provided golden opportunities for SYNCHROVEST!

You could, if you prefer, choose a closed-end investment trust such as Tri-Continental or Lehman for your vehicle. These trusts, like Mutual Funds, own stock portfolios; but unlike Funds they do not stand ready to redeem your shares. You must buy and sell them through your broker like any other stock. Another difference is that the price per share of these trusts rarely reflects its true value. At times, an investment trust share may sell at a discount, at other times at a premium—whatever price the public is willing to pay for it at any given time. Presently, most closed-ends are selling at discounts with the result that investors can buy "more stock" for their money and receive higher dividends than they ordinarily would.

For most of us, there is more to life than the fatiguing, self-deluding, futile attempt to outsmart the experts. SYNCHROVEST gives us the time to smell the flowers. Penn State football coach Joe Paterno put it this way a couple of Januarys back in Miami, when amazed reporters asked him why he terminated his practice sessions at noon to let his players swim, frolic in the sun, and stay out late at night when they were presently going to have to face a dangerous herd of stampeding steers from Kansas: "I think a bowl trip should be a reward, not a punishment. This is a once-in-a-lifetime thing for most of these kids. How often are you good enough to play in the Orange Bowl? We're down here to win a football game. But there is more to life than just hard work." Joe's boys beat Kansas—as they have just about every other team they've played in recent memory—so taking time to smell the flowers might not be such a dangerous business philosophy at that.

SYNCHROVEST can be your master plan for no-sweat financial security and peace of mind. Automatically obviated are anxieties over recessions, the price of gold, the supply of gold, the balance of payments, the gross national product, wholesale prices, retail sales, the Phillips curve, tight money, interest rates, inflation, lower corporate profits, higher taxes, selling climaxes, government controls, the three-leg theory of bear markets, whether you really are a masochist because you keep losing or whether it just salves the croupier's conscience to *say* you are as he takes your money, declines in personal income, Keynesians, neo-Keynesians, non-Keynesians, and all the rest of that enervating economic omphaloskepsis. In a very real sense, you are not investing in a stock at all, or even in the stock market in the traditional sense, but in a mathematical formula predicated on historical probability and reinforced by a currently valid premise, videlicet, that the market will come back! And if the government puts the boots to the internal combustion engine, grounds the airlines, and stops the food industry from dumping risky BHT—butylatedhydroxyltoluene—into children's breakfast cereals as England did, you should worry? You should not worry because something else will come along and take their places and the market will come back. And as for the vehicle itself, it really isn't of paramount importance *which* you ride. All will fluctuate, and no one knows now what next year's big winner will be in individual stocks or Mutual Funds. The ten best performing Mutual Funds of this year, for example, will certainly not repeat as the top ten next year. Indeed, it would be surprising if *one* of them reappeared in next year's select group.

Here are the top ten Funds of 1968—and how they ranked the following year.

1968 RANK	1969 RANK
1. Neuwirth Fund	259
2. Gibraltar Growth	169
3. Mates Investment	307
4. First Sierra Fund	77
5. Pennsylvania Mutual	328
6. Puerto Rican Inv.	30
7. Crown-West.-Dallas	279
8. Franklin Dynatech	337
9. First Participating	49
10. Enterprise Fund	329

Any two years would tell a similar story, but 1968-1969 is the most recent two-year period in which we have an up-year followed by a down-year, as measured by the Dow Jones Average—a mild rise in 1968, a mild decline in 1969.

The most recent two-year period, 1971 and 1972, both registered gains; and even here, under roughly similar conditions, not one of the top 10 performing funds of 1971 repeated in the following year.

1971	GAIN
1. Nicholas Strong	86%
2. 44 Wall Street	71%
3. Afuture	67%
4. Channing Venture	61%
5. Rowe Price New Horizons	52%
6. Redmond Growth Fund	49%
7. IDS New Dimen.	48%
8. GAC Growth Fund	48%
9. R.S. Hershey Fund	47%
10. Torrence Eq. Fund	47%
DOW JONES AVERAGE	6%

1972	GAIN
1. Templeton Growth	68%
2. International Investors	58%
3. Am. Insurance and Ind.	45%
4. Omega Fund	44%
5. Twentieth Century Gr.	42%
6. Putnam Voyager	41%
7. Charter Fund	37%
8. Putnam Vista	36%
9. Janus Fund	34%
10. Life Ins. Investors	34%
DOW JONES AVERAGE	15%

All this is just a way of emphasizing that with SYNCHROVEST there is no real necessity to try to pick next year's standout—even if it were possible. It is *fluctuation*, the one element common to every security, that will enable you to achieve superior results.

Human nature being what it is, the mass of investors rushes to buy when the market seems to be heading perpetually upward, and yet this is precisely the riskiest time for the average investor. He accumulates shares at ever-dearer prices, rendering himself increasingly more vulnerable to the inevitable downturn. Lucretius observed some two thousand years ago: "For we see that anything is more quickly destroyed than again renewed" *Verus*. In the space of months—even weeks—the stock market can plummet to levels from which it had begun its long, apparently endless climb several years earlier. And after the disenchantment and the bitterness have faded, the investor once again tilts an attentive ear toward the Sirens of the Street and the mystical, seductive song they sing.

If SYNCHROVEST does nothing but stop our ears from hearing that song, it will have performed an invaluable function indeed.

NOTE:

Many brokerage houses offer the New York Stock Exchange's Monthly Investment Plan (MIP) in which, for as little as forty dollars a month, an investor may accumulate stock in any company listed on the New York Stock Exchange. Such a plan lends itself to use with SYNCHROVEST, and all transactions can be conveniently handled by mail. Some brokers, such as Merrill Lynch, Pierce, Fenner & Smith Inc., which calls its MIP Plan "Special Investor Accounts," prepare a list of stocks from the New York Stock Exchange that has been approved by their Research Department—thus helping you with your selection. Dividends can be reinvested automatically.

Commissions run high on small purchases of stock, but the bank interest you will receive on your SYNCHROVEST *Credit Balance Account* should more than compensate for them over a period of time.

8 *The De-Greening of America —And How to Be on the Winning Side Next Time!*

In the entire investment community, there is probably no dispute of longer standing or hotter temperature than that between investors who believe that short-term investing is the royal road to riches in the stock market, and investors who insist that greater profits are piled up over the long term. Short-termers remind us that stocks crashed in 1929 and meted a quick and merciful death to their brethren, but long-term investors, cautious men who believed in the long-term future of the U.S. economy and had their money invested in solid blue chip companies, were hung by their heels and slowly drained off up to 90% of their blood in the following three years.

Short-termers think that long-term investing is a cop-out, a hedge against ignorance, and that investment companies and other money managers who say they are investing for long-term growth are confessing their lack of knowledge, their laziness, or their market incompetence, and are hoping that if they simply buy the respectable stuff and hang onto it, time will bail them out.

Though long-termers preach safety as a prime benefit of their method, short-termers claim their way actually offers less risk. "We cut and run," says one of the most successful traders I know—and there aren't many. "We buy a stock and if it doesn't behave right we dump it, chalk it up to life, and go on to something else. But the long-termers just have to grit their teeth and hang on. Trading has a way of hoisting the warning flag. You buy a stock and it bombs. You buy another stock and it bombs. You do this a few times and you get the hint that either you've lost your touch or the market is trying to tell you something.

"The average investor doesn't stand a chance. To be a successful trader, you have to be a born gambler. You have to be able to take a big loss as fast and as easily as you take a big gain. You treat a stock like a playboy treats a woman. You make a pitch, and if she doesn't go for it, fine, goodbye, there's plenty more around. If she goes for it, dandy, you hang around until her looks fade or something better comes along and you dump her. You have to make it a full-time job. You have to have access to good information, have a sixth sense, and you have to be lucky.

"What your average lunch-hour gunslinger doesn't realize is, if you miss the top by only 10% and the bottom by only 10%, and add in your buying and selling commissions, hell, you need a swing of about 25% in a stock just to break even. You luck out a few times with that kind of handicap and you're in deep, deep trouble. And don't forget, we have to pay full income tax on our profit, whereas the long-termer can cut it in half."

Most successful traders admit that luck plays a major role in their business. But luck is not a thing that can be acquired. Jesse Livermore, one of America's most famous stock market speculators, expressed it this way: "When a man has lived by luck, he lives with fear. If luck departs, where do you go for a new supply?" After Livermore's own luck departed, he shot himself.

Luck plays a lesser role in the life of the long-term investor. Historically, our economy has constantly expanded, and all evidence points to continued expansion. Time will probably bail out the long-termer if he selects a variety of good, substantial stocks and locks them up.

The long-termer has a couple of other good things going for him. He gets socked with the same commission as the short-termer when he buys a stock, but he pays it only once. The trader may go in and out of the same stock half a dozen times in the course of a year trying to pump himself some profits. If the pump's primed and he gets a gush, he doesn't mind giving his broker a drink of his nectar. If not, the broker drinks while the trader goes dry.

Second, dividends are of no importance to the trader. He may be in and out of that stock numerous times in a year and still miss out on the dividends, simply because he was not a "shareholder of record" on the dividend date. That doesn't concern him. A dividend of 3% or 4% isn't going to make that much difference in his year-end results.

The long-termer, on the other hand, gets those checks as regularly as clockwork; and as the economy grows and his companies prosper, the dividend checks may get larger and larger. He may eventually find that he is no longer receiving a yield of 3% or 4% on his original investment, but twice or three times that. Such a "bonus" goes far to help ease the anxiety of the long-termer who is "locked in" during a long bear market.

For if he is now receiving a yield of 10% on his original investment, he'll recoup his entire investment in ten years come hell or high water, not to mention the dividends he has already received over the years. So whatever the stock will be worth ten years from now, he's pretty secure. When the trader loses, he loses. He can't patiently refill his glass with the drip, drip, drip of dividends because he doesn't own a piece of the cow.

Have a statistic: The 100 richest companies in the U.S. in 1945 did pretty well on average for their shareholders who bought and held on for the next twenty years. IBM did the best. Its stock increased 5,350%! Schenley Industries did the worst, losing 43%. Yet, the unluckiest juicehead, who picked Schenley over IBM, still did not actually lose a penny of his money, for he received much more than 43% in dividends. And time bailed him out, too, for Schenley sobered up *after* 1965 and flew like a bird. Not all investors in 1945 who simply packed their portfolios with a selection of stocks of the 100 top companies may have included IBM, but they had a very good chance of picking any number of stocks that turned in excellent performances, such as Kodak, Texaco, and Eastern Gas and Fuel, all of which gained more than 1,000%.

Lots of little old ladies have a million bucks in dusty stocks locked up in safe deposit vaults—but most traders still die broke.

Yes . . . but by May of 1970 the stock market had plunged to its lowest level in more than seven years. The de-greening of America took just eighteen months during which the Dow Jones Industrial Average dropped some 354 points—more than a third! Countless other stocks, listed and unlisted, lost much more than that; and even some Mutual Funds had dived twice that far. In the worst bear market since the depression, the big and the little watched their investments being hammered to pieces under the almost daily bludgeonings in

Wall Street. M. Ross Perot, president and largest stockholder of Electronic Data Systems, saw his own investment drop $445 million in a single day when the price of his company's stock tumbled 50 points. Mrs. Smith watched her $3,000 in a Mutual Fund dwindle away to $1,500—50%—and realized with a shock that the stock would have to go up 100% for her to break even.

It is safe to speculate that 1970 did for many investors what 1962 almost did: drove them permanently out of the market, broke, bitter and betrayed. Most keenly disappointed, perhaps, were the conservative investors who really hadn't been greedy, who really hadn't asked for much. To what end, then, the long, patient years of Dollar Cost Averaging, watching the shares multiply, watching the price edge upward, slowly dwarfing the original price—and now finally plunging *below* the starting price and dragging great numbers of high-priced shares down with them.

But 1969-70 provided exciting opportunities for those who understood that bear markets are shorter than bull markets and that sharply increased buying must occur in these periods if they are to build a massive pyramid. Though the total net assets of most Mutual Funds plunged in 1970, some, either because of the reputation of their managements or because investors felt they were more dependable, actually increased their total net assets! Year-old Rowe Price New Era Fund, for example, no world-beater during its first year of operation, actually doubled its assets in 1970—from $43 million to $89 million—even though its price per share was going down!

These investors would understand what SYNCHROVEST is all about. And so would money-managers. Says New Era's President Howard P. Colhoun, "Net redemptions can force fund managers to liquidate holdings which they may otherwise prefer to keep. Positive sales, on the other hand, allow fund managers to take advantage of individual investment opportunities as they occur."

It is no secret that the abysmal record of many Funds in the '70 crash was due as much to the behavior of their panicked shareholders demanding their money as it was to the investment decisions of their managers.

After the collapse of '70, the T. Rowe Price Growth Stock Fund—the nation's largest No-Load—took a look at the damage done to its 15 largest holdings. This is what they saw:

	1968-70 High	Price 6/30/70
Xerox	116	73
IBM	387	250
Polaroid	146	53
Warner-Lambert	76	61
Philip Morris	39	36
Coca-Cola	87	69
Texas Instruments	140	74
Avon Products	92	70
Walt Disney	158	117
General Electric	100	68
Eastman Kodak	87	64
Combined Insurance	72	44
Minn. Mining & Mfg.	120	76
Avery Products	42	26
PepsiCo	57	44

The worst bear market in more than thirty years had taken its toll.

But then the Price people decided to compare the prices of these same stocks at their *1962* low with their prices after the *1970* crash:

	1962 Low	Price 6/30/70
Xerox	6	73
IBM	78	250
Polaroid	10	53
Warner-Lambert	17	61
Philip Morris	10	36
Coca-Cola	18	69
Texas Instruments	20	74
Avon Products	10	70
Walt Disney	9	117
General Electric	54	68
Eastman Kodak	20	64
Combined Insurance	7	44
Minn. Mining & Mfg.	41	76
Avery Products	2	26
PepsiCo	17	44

"Why do most people want to buy stocks after they have experienced big advances in a bull market and lose their nerve and want to sell after an extended bear market?" the Price people ask. It was a rhetorical question; the answer is as old as the stock market.

Another question could have been asked: "Why is the securities market the only market in the world where customers flock to buy at inflated prices but stay at home when bargain sales are held?" The answer, of course, is greed and fear—greed at the top and fear at the bottom. The emotions are natural and rational enough, *but they've been inverted.* It should be fear at the top and greed at the bottom, but because we have been programmed to respond incorrectly, the proper order does not compute. The very few people who have mastered the market have first mastered themselves, altered their circuitry to elicit the correct response. SYNCHROVEST does this for you automatically!

Were it not for the roiling backwash of the falls, the salmon would be unable to propel himself twenty miles an hour out of the water and scale the falls on his odyssey homeward to the placid lake. *The turmoil supplies the thrust—just as SYNCHROVEST uses the backwash of a tumbling market for the giant leap upward.*

If you can't buy low and sell high—and who can with any consistency?—well, then, buy low and sell low. A teratoid heresy? If you had purchased the stocks shown in the T. Rowe Price chart (or any number of others) at their 1962 lows and sold them at their 1970 lows, the Internal Revenue Service would receive you with open arms. The Synchrovestor would automatically have purchased a large amount of stock at the '62 low, and from the crest of the market in December 1968, until the mid-'70 nadir, he had a year and a half in which to decide whether to take profits or ride her down into the backwash again for the next leap upward.

That is the Magic of SYNCHROVEST.

Don't Miss Out on an Interest of 250 to 1,000% Per Annum on Your U.S. Savings Bonds

9

In November of 1969 the U.S. Senate gave the American people an early Christmas present by passing a bill raising the interest on U.S. Savings Bonds from 4¼% to 5%. It was the first time bonds have paid more than 4¼% since the Liberty Act of 1918. In 1967 the Treasury did begin issuing "Freedom Shares" bearing a higher interest rate than 4¼%, but made them available only to those buying regular bonds under payroll savings or bond-a-month plans. Purchase was limited to $1.08 worth of "Freedom Shares" for each $1.00 of regular Savings Bonds acquired.

Even a citizen with a totally flat EEG (electroencephalogram) knew that the Senate was not motivated by the goodwill of the season, but by a genuine desire to arrest the redemption rate of Savings Bonds, which had been climbing alarmingly over the past several years—exceeding purchases for months at a time—as the nation's savers switched their idle funds into higher-yielding investments.

Historically, the U.S. has not been counted among the most generous of governments in paying its citizens for the use of their money, having relied mainly on pitches of patriotism to induce purchases of Savings Bonds—the pitchman, generally, is an overpaid celeb whose money manager would recoil in horror if his client were really serious. But a public becoming increasingly more sophisticated financially was not buying anymore. Too many respected investment advisors and such were calling Savings Bonds a "swindle" and an investment palmed off mostly on financial rubes.

To an extent, the critics were right. With a higher interest rate available from banks, bonds were not a financially attractive proposition. But now, thanks to another increase, Savings Bonds pay an interest rate of 5½% when held to their maturity of 5 years and 10 months, making them more competitive with banks and savings and loan associations.* Regular passbook rates range from 5% at commercial banks to 5¼% at savings banks and savings and loan associations. The new guaranteed rate certificates pay considerably more.

Besides being a good way to save for those who lack the discipline to save regularly, or the will power to leave their savings alone, Savings Bonds contain a built-in advantage that is generally overlooked. That advantage, coupled with their higher interest, is sufficient to warrant a closer look at Savings Bonds as a savings medium.

First, although the interest on Savings Bonds is taxable, the government permits the bondholder to defer his taxes until he cashes in his bond. Thus, a taxpayer can hold the bond until his retirement—when he will normally find himself in a lower tax bracket—or until he runs into a bad year, income-wise. Either way, he'll pay less tax on the interest than he would

*At press time the interest rate on Savings Bonds was raised to 6%.

otherwise—and less tax than the saver who puts his money in a bank and has to declare the interest every year on his income tax form.

The wage earner in, say, a 36% tax bracket, deludes himself if he thinks he is getting 5½% interest on his money, because out of every $5.50 he receives from the bank, he must pay the tax man $1.98. The saver *actually* receives only $3.52—3½%—on his money.

The second advantage—one even less recognized than the first—is that U.S. Savings Bonds are exempt from state and city income taxes. In many turnip-tapping areas, these levies could add several more percentage points to his total income tax bill so that he'll have to surrender more of those interest dollars.

In order to realize a true interest of 5½%, the wage earner in a 36% bracket would need to earn 8.59% on his money! And before you blithely glide by that statement with the consoling thought that *you* aren't in the 36% bracket or anywhere near it, are you sure? Do you really know what tax bracket you're in? You might be in for a surprise. Check the tax rate schedules in your income tax forms. On the schedule you used to figure your income tax, find the line that applied to you. There is a percentage figure in the third column of this line (introduced by a plus sign) that tells you precisely what your income tax bracket is. If you were a single taxpayer whose taxable income in 1972 was $14,100, the percentage figure given is 31%. And if you pay state and/or city income tax as well, you must repeat the same procedures with those schedules, then add them to the Federal figure. If, for example, you are in the 31% Federal tax bracket, the 7% state bracket, and the 2% city income tax bracket, your true income tax bracket is 40%—and in order for you to have been able to pocket 5½% interest on your savings, you would have had to *earn* more than 9% on your money! For every $5.50 you earned from a bank, the government allowed you to keep only $3.30!

The table below shows the interest rates wage earners in various tax brackets would have to earn to be able to *keep* 5½%.

TAX BRACKET	INTEREST RATE NEEDED
22	7.05
25	7.33
28	7.64
32	8.09
36	8.59
39	9.02
42	9.48
45	10.00
48	10.58
50	11.00
53	11.70
55	12.22
58	13.10
60	13.75
62	14.47
64	15.28
66	16.18
68	17.19
69	17.74
70	18.33

Neither Savings Bonds nor banks are a good investment in the sense that you can make money in them. With the cost of living rising as it has, the best that can be hoped for is that your saved dollar will be worth as much when you take it out as when you put it in.

Then why save in either one? The answer is simple: You've got to put it *somewhere.* Every family must have a reserve of cash for emergencies, and these are good places to keep it. As to which one is better, the answer depends on individual circumstances. A retired or disabled person with limited income would do better in savings banks: the interest rate is higher, and he'd pay little or no tax on it. The average working person is probably better off putting his emergency funds into Savings Bonds. He can defer taxes on them, and if he suddenly loses his income due to illness or loss of job, he can cash in his bonds as he needs them, collect all the interest, and pay little or no tax on it in that lean year. Granted, tax exempt municipal bonds pay similar interest that is *totally* tax free; but these are not as safe as Savings Bonds, require specialized knowledge, cannot be purchased or redeemed as conveniently, are not available in such a wide variety of denominations, demand more care and attention, and cost commission charges to buy and sell.

Viewed in this light, savings accounts are more of a swindle and an investment for rubes than Savings Bonds. As has happened with other investments in the past, the little guy who bought Bonds may end up outsmarting the experts.

A word of caution here concerning the high interest rates now being offered by banks on their "Time Savings Accounts," "Guaranteed Rate Accounts," and "Certificates of Deposit." As of July 1, 1973, the banking authorities have permitted an escalation of interest which, on the surface, appears to be a bonanza for savers. But concealed in this bouquet of dazzling rates is a thorn that could draw more blood than you might realize: *FDIC regulations permit withdrawals on Time Savings Accounts prior to maturity provided rate of interest on amount withdrawn is reduced to pass book rate and 3 months' interest is forfeited.*

What this means to you is that, regardless of how long you have held the certificate, if you withdraw from it before the maturity date, the bank will pay you only its regular pass book rate on this withdrawal for all the time it has been on deposit, *and* will penalize you three months' interest on this money to boot!

Thus, if you own a $5,000 4-year certificate paying 7.75% (with an effective yield of 8.17%), and cash it in after two years, the bank will not give you the $850 your certificate has earned at 8.17% interest, but only $562—interest at the regular pass book rate of 5¼% (an effective yield of 5.47%). Further, you must also forfeit three months' earnings—$68—for a total penalty of $356! This represents a rip-off of 6% from the value of your account. Viewed another way, the penalty amounts to more than 7% of your original $5,000.

The same account cashed in after three years will be penalized a stunning $530—$462 representing the difference in interest between 8.17% and 5.47%, plus the three month penalty of $68! This amounts to a plundering of more than 8% in your account—*or 11% of your original deposit!*

I will spare you the shock of what would happen to you if your deposit was even larger—or if you purchased a certificate with a 7-year maturity date and cashed it in after six years or so!

Small wonder that at least one bank cautioned its depositors that the penalties are severe.

The new certificates are attractive, true, but be very, very careful when you buy one that you will not have to redeem it before maturity.

Let's briefly examine the rates being offered by savings banks and savings and loan associations.

Regular pass book account:	5.25%
1-2½ year certificates:	6.50%
2½-4 year certificates:	6.75%
4-7 year certificates:	7.00%
4-7 year certificates (minimum deposit may range from $2,500 to $5,000):	7.75%

Which is the best buy? How much better are the higher-yielding Time Certificates than the regular pass book account, which imposes no penalty for withdrawal?

If you agree to tie your money up for 1 year, you can get 6.50%—24% more return on your money!

If you tied your money up for 2½ years, you can get 6.75%. You will receive only 29% more return on your money than you would at the pass book rate of 5¼%—and you have substantially increased the likelihood that you will have to cash in prior to maturity and pay the penalty.

If you tied your money up for 4 years, you can get 7%—33% more interest than the pass book rate. But is it really worth tying up your money for 4 years, with its high risk of having to cash in somewhere along the way, when the 1-year certificate offers you 24% more than the passbook account? You will be getting only about 8% more dollars than in the 1-year certificate.

The 7.75% certificate is more interesting, representing, as it does, a 48% increase over the regular pass book rate and offering 20% more dollars than the 1-year certificate.

But the caveat still applies: be sure you won't have to touch this money prior to maturity!

Thc best buy? For those who are positive they will *not* have to withdraw prior to maturity, the 7.75% certificate appears most attractive. For those not so positive, and for those who suspect interest rates might go up in the future and who do not want to be locked in at 7.75%, when banks may be offering even higher rates later on, the 1-year certificate is a most appealing compromise.

Of course, you still must pay income taxes on your interest! Which brings us back to Savings Bonds.

Many a millionaire would consider the perfect investment to be one which offered absolute safety of his principal and would return to him, ten, twenty or thirty years hence, the exact purchasing power of the dollars he had put in. Because of their exemption from evergrowing state and city income taxes, and their Federal tax deferral feature, the lowly, laughable U.S. Savings Bond—particularly if inflation remains within control—could conceivably turn out to be just that.

MONEY-MAKING BONUS #1! Since the issue date of U.S. Savings Bonds is always the first day of the month in which you buy them, make your purchases on the last day of the month and you'll get a month's free interest!

MONEY-MAKING BONUS #2: Most holders of Series E Savings Bonds make a crucial error when they redeem their bonds and unknowingly deprive themselves of an annual interest rate of up to 1,000%! You read correctly—1,000%! Your banker won't warn you because the odds are that *he doesn't know,* just as most bankers believe that Savings Bonds, like any other bond, pay interest only on the principal—certainly not on the accumulated interest. But a glance at the 1972 increase in value of mature $1,000 Series E Bonds purchased in any December since 1942 shows a jump *in value* during 1972 of between 5.10% and 6.46%! If interest were paid only on the principal of these bonds—$750—the dollar increase in value during 1972 would amount to an interest of between 7.73% and 17.12%! A $1,000 bond purchased for $750 in December of 1942, for example, was worth $1,986 in December of 1971 and $2,114.40 a year later in December of 1972. This represents an increase for the year of $128.40, 6.46% more than the preceding year—but it is also an increase of 17.12% of the original principal of the bond!

Suppose, like many Americans, you cashed in a Savings Bond in December of 1972 to help pay Christmas bills. Let's say it was a $1,000 bond you purchased in May of 1952. On

Friday, December 29th, you walked into your bank, redeemed the bond, and walked out with $1,569.60. Perhaps you congratulated yourself on doubling your money. Perhaps you even knew you were receiving $90 more than you would have had you cashed it in last December—an increase of 6.08%. But had you waited only until the next business day to redeem your bond—January 2nd—you would have received not $1,569.60, but $1,612.80! The extra $43.20 would have represented an annual interest rate for those four days of 251%! If December 31st had fallen, say, on a Monday, you could have redeemed your bond the day after New Year's and received, for those two days, an annual interest rate of 502%! In other months, merely by waiting one day until the first of the next month, you can draw interest for that day at the astronomical annual rate of 1,004%!

In the first example, you received $43.20 for four days—$10.80 a day. On a yearly basis, the interest at that rate would amount to $3,942 for 365 days (365 X $10.80). This is 251% of your principal—the $1,569.60 your bond was worth only four days earlier.

In the second case, you received $43.20 for waiting only two days—$21.60 per day. Multiply 365 by $21.60 and the result is $7,884.00—equal to 502% interest on your principal.

In the third case, you received your $43.20 for waiting only a single day. On a yearly basis at this rate, your return would be $15,768.00 (365 X $43.20)—an interest of 1,004%!

It is important, then, before presenting your bond for redemption, to find out when interest will next be credited to your bond. Your banker is supplied with redemption tables in advance and will tell you if you ask him. *Remember that interest is not credited to every bond on the same month.* A $1,000 bond purchased in July, August, September, or October of 1952—the same year in which you purchased *your* bond—did not increase at all in January of 1973, nor in February either for that matter. Interest on Savings Bonds is credited semi-annually.

When you need money, don't select a bond at random for redemption. Find out which one will increase in value on the first of the following month and redeem *that* one on the first!

Many people make the mistake of cashing in a Savings Bond when it is "almost" mature, believing that the few weeks or months remaining before maturity will not account for all that much interest. This is a critical error. The interest rate, starting as it did at 4% in the first year and climbing slowly during subsequent years, must begin to hustle as the bond nears maturity if the bondholder is to realize an overall annual yield of 5½% for each of those years. Therefore, in the final four months before maturity (presently 5 years and 10 months) Savings Bonds leap in value 5%—an annual interest rate of 15%!

Worse, if you redeem your bond four months and one day before maturity, you will miss out on *two* big interest dates, which would have skyrocketed the value of your bond a full 8%—*or a lip-biting annual interest rate for the period of 24%!*

10 How to Make Up to 44% Per Year on Your Savings —Guaranteed by the U.S. Government

By combining the purchase or sale of U.S. Savings Bonds with a bank account, you can walk out of the bank with many times the interest you normally would have coming to you—and nobody will even shoot you. Here's how:

Buy your bonds on the last month of a quarter and you can pick up *extra* interest of more than 11% per annum for that month:

- Dec. 1 Deposit, say, $750 in a day-of-deposit-to-day-of-withdrawal account.
- Dec. 10 Withdraw the $750 and deposit in a regular savings account offering 10 grace days.
- Dec. 31 Withdraw the $750 and buy a $1,000 bond.

You'll get 10 days interest on your day-of-deposit account,

one month's interest on your regular account, and one month's interest on your Savings Bond—a total annual interest rate of more than 11%!

The same bonus interest is available to you when you redeem your bonds on the last month of a quarter:

Dec. 1 Redeem bond, deposit funds in day-of-deposit-to-day-of-withdrawal account.
Dec. 10 Withdraw funds and deposit in a regular savings account offering 10 grace days.
Dec. 31 Withdraw funds and buy bond.

If your redemption date happened to coincide with the regular increase in the value of your Savings Bonds, you could quadruple that bonus! Here's how:

	INTEREST
Value of Savings Bond Nov. 30: $1,000	
Value of Savings Bond Dec. 1: $1,027.50	$27.50
10 days bank interest on $1027.50	1.46
One month bank interest on $1027.50	4.54
One month interest on new Savings Bonds purchased with available funds	3.51
Total	$37.01

Total earnings for December of $37.01 represent an incredible annual interest rate of 44.41%!

These results are obtainable even at commercial banks that pay only 5% on savings accounts. But because savings banks and savings and loan associations pay 5¼%, the extra ¼ of 1% plus continuous compounding will increase the results given.

How to Play the Credit Card Game —And Make Money Doing It! 11

Consumers resort to all sorts of ruses to buy themselves time from the bill collector. Some of them are legal, others quasi-legal, a few are definitely no-no's. All appear to be execrable—until one takes into account the draconian measures employed by some businesses to collect those bills: threatening computer-letters, nationwide credit blacklisting, salary garnishment, humiliation created by interviewing the debtor's neighbors, and the angry voice on the telephone conjuring up images of cement footwear and deep water. In that light, some debt-dodging devices can at least be understood, if not forgiven; and there are times, particularly when the consumer has paid his bill on time but continues to be dunned by TOM, that Thoroughly Obedient Moron called a computer, that the ruses can be viewed as nothing more than self-defense.

Among the Fabian tactics in the consumer game-book:

• Leave unopened letters in your mailbox and claim you've been out of town. You aren't legally required to open your mail.

• Burn the bills and say they somehow got thrown out with all the junk mail you get.

• If the voice on the telephone threatens to haul you into court and the bill you owe is less than $100, tell him, "OK by me. Let me know the court date." Most bill collectors won't go to court to collect that amount—it doesn't pay.

• When you can't stall any longer, tell them you *sent* the check and it must have gone astray in the mail. Tell them that if the check doesn't arrive shortly, you'll cancel it and send another one. This dodge is especially effective with the telephone company, its practitioners claim, as it keeps your phone working and permits you to run up even higher bills before you have to take action one way or the other.

• Send $10 a month to each one of your creditors as evidence of your intention to pay. This may keep them off your back for awhile. Caution: If the firm uses a computer, this dodge will not compute. The Thoroughly Obedient Moron will dun you for the balance.

• When everything else fails, send your creditor a check—but don't sign it. This ploy will buy you up to a couple of weeks' time. And if you need a couple of weeks more, sign your checks but send each of them to the wrong creditor.

• Put a staple through your check to delay processing of your check by the bank's computer.

• Smear a small dab of vaseline over the code numerals on your check to slow down the bank's magnetic encoding machine.

• Threaten to go bankrupt and deprive your creditor of the entire amount you owe unless he'll chop the bill down to an amount you can afford to pay.

• Go bankrupt. Some 200,000 consumers do every year. Don't believe the myth that your credit will be wrecked permanently. If you have a steady job, you may find you're a good credit risk again shortly after bankruptcy.

Whether all these credit dodges work is a matter for speculation, but the author's reaction to them is probably the same as yours: initial amusement followed by a feeling of disgust at deadbeats who pervert the whole system of credit, display bad faith, and make it rougher on the rest of us by forcing *us* to pick up the tab to cover losses *they* cause.

Besides, it doesn't show cleverness, it shows ignorance. Why go to such absurd, risky, and self-demeaning lengths to delay the day of reckoning for a week or two when a credit card offers you, legally, nearly two months of grace on your bills without your having to indulge in any kind of machination at all! And without costing you a cent!

Credit cards bill you once a month for the purchases you've run up the preceding month. The billing date varies among the various cards available. Assume it's the first of the month. The purchases you made on the first of the preceding month are just now being billed to you—30 days later. On top of that, the credit card company allows you 25 more days in which to pay before it begins to add interest!

There is the kind of fellow who calls his wife from the bar phone and, when she answers, gives her the first three digits of the phone he's calling from and hangs up. He gets his dime back because the phone company allows a couple of seconds before it claims the dime permanently. He then calls her back, gives her the remaining digits of his phone, hangs up, and pockets the dime that clinks down the coin chute. Now that she knows his number, his wife calls him from her home phone and they talk for free. The fellow say he'll be home shortly, then returns to the bar and spends another five bucks on booze before hitting the road. This kind of fellow will take advantage of his credit card's "grace period" and delay paying his bill until the last minute.

The more astute individual, recognizing that time is money, will use that "grace period" to put dollars into his pocket. He uses his credit card to make purchases, but pays cash for whatever he buys. Only he doesn't pay the cash to the merchant—he deposits it in his savings account! Thus, when it comes time to pay his bill to the credit card company, this individual may already have earned nearly two months' interest on the money—money that's not even his! On a thousand dollars, he'll earn about $8 interest—and if you don't think that's much money, try borrowing it. For that matter, try working for it. If you're in the 50% bracket, you must earn $16 to go home with $8. That's not right, is it? You would have to earn *more* than $16 to go home with $8, because we have not deducted the *cost* of earning that $16—transportation to and from work, lunches, clothes, dry cleaning, etc. Moreover, that $8 is yours forever; it will go on earning interest for you, year after year, for as long as you let it.

One credit card is sufficient if you arrange to make your largest purchases around the same date each month (the date farthest from your billing date), but with four or five credit cards, each with different billing dates, you could always make your purchases with the card whose billing date is farthest away. To simplify: Each Monday morning before leaving for work, select the proper card and carry that one throughout the week. The money you will save, and the interest that money will earn, can amount to thousands of dollars over the years—thousands of dollars of found money!

But all bills must eventually be paid—and if they aren't paid on time, the credit card people hit you with an awesome interest rate of 18% per annum. That must be avoided like the plague, and one way to do it if you don't have sufficient cash in your checking account is through the use of the charter check credit or cash reserve account offered by many banks. With such an account, the bank permits you to write a "bad" check—that is, a check in excess of your bank balance—but instead of bouncing it as the bank ordinarily would when the check comes through to clear, the bank graciously digs into its own pocket (to a maximum of $1,000 typically) and makes it good. But this overdraft is a loan, and the bank charges you about 12% per year for it. True, this interest is a third less than the credit card company demands, but you will never get rich paying 12% for money. Far better to withdraw the money from your savings account to pay the bill if it comes to that. You'll lose the 5% interest your money would have earned, but you'll avoid the 18% you would have had to pay the credit card company—*a net saving to you on your credit card interest charges of 72%!*

12 How to Get 100 Bank Gifts for the Same Deposit!

Imagine a stock that is selling at $50 a share. You can buy it without any sales commission whatever. It is guaranteed to perform, year after year, the way you see it here; and it is further guaranteed that it will never, at any time, "go South," as they say on Wall Street: it *cannot* go down, it can only go up! And at the end of the 7th year, it is guaranteed to yield a dividend of 12% on your original investment!

1st year:	53 5/8
2nd year:	57 5/8
3rd year:	61 7/8
4th year:	66 3/8
5th year:	71 1/4
6th year:	76 1/2
7th year:	82 1/8
8th year:	88 1/4
9th year:	94 3/4
10th year:	101 5/8

Interested? In view of what has happened to many unguaranteed stocks in the past, many people might hail this as the investment of a lifetime. But it isn't a stock at all; it's a 7% savings certificate available at any savings bank—with an effective annual yield of 7.35%, thanks to continuous compounding of interest. It can be purchased in any denomination from $1,000 up, but every $50 of your money will perform exactly as indicated here. And, although most banks will guarantee this interest rate for only seven years, some savings and loan institutions, like California Federal Savings, *will* guarantee it for ten years.

But now, as attractive as the 7% rate may appear, many banks have added a sweetener in the form of free gifts as an added inducement to get your savings. In return for the gift, the bank requires that you leave your money on deposit for a period of 12 to 14 months. Banks give gifts with a retail value of about $10 for a deposit of $500, and gifts which sell for about $20 for a $5,000 deposit.

In addition, many banks offer gifts with a retail value below $10 for lesser deposits of $250, $200, $100, and even $50. You can't get a 7% account for such small deposits, but you do get 5¼%.

The only drawback to the 7% free-gift account is that it ties your money up for a year or so—but *any* 7% account, with or without gifts, ties your money up for a minimum of four years. If you withdraw from your nongift 7% account before maturity, the bank will not give you the 7% interest these funds have already earned, but only the regular pass book rate (currently 5¼%)—and you will also have to forfeit three months' interest on these funds. So if you closed your $5,000 nongift account after one year, say, you lose 1¾% (the difference between 7% and 5¼%) plus three months' penalty—about 1⅓%—for a grand total of some 3%. A solid loss of $150!

If you withdraw prematurely from your free-gift 7% account, you must also pay the bank back the cost of the gift (about $10 for the $5,000 gift and $5 for the $500 category gift). Thus, if you close your $5,000 free gift account before the 12 or 14 month waiting period is up, your loss rises to about 3¼%.

And if you close your $500 6¾% free-gift account after 1 year, before its 2½ year maturity and before the gift waiting period is up, you will be penalized 3.8%—$19.00 (2.8% of $500.00 plus $5 for the gift, which amounts to 1%).

There is no penalty for withdrawal from an ordinary 5¼% account—but if it's a gift account and you close it before the end of the waiting period, you owe the bank the cost of the gift, typically under $5.

Now obviously 7% is better than 5¼%, and a gift worth $20 better than a gift worth $10. But if you can get a $10 gift for $500 on a 6¾% account, why would you want to deposit ten times that amount for a gift worth only two times as much? In short, a $20 gift for a $5,000 7% account represents a "bonus" of only 4/10 of 1% on your money; but a $10 gift on $500 works out to a full 2%! You will be getting 8¾% on your money (6¾% + 2%) for that first year!

On the surface, the $500 6¾% account seems to be the best deal in the free-gift sweepstakes—but look closer. Gifts being offered for deposits of only $100 and $50 in 5¼% accounts average about $5 in value so if, instead of depositing $5,000 and receiving a $20 gift, you opened 50 $100 accounts, you would receive 50 $5 gifts—$250 in merchandise! You would receive only 5¼% interest on your money, but the $250 in merchandise represents a bonus interest of another 5%, for a total of 10¼%!

And if you open 100, free-gift, $50 accounts, the $5 gift

would amount to a bonus of 10% on your 5¼% account—a grand total of 15¼%! And you would be getting 100 bank gifts instead of one—$500 worth of merchandise!

You don't need all that merchandise? Give them for Christmas, birthday, housewarming and wedding presents—which you'd have to buy anyway. It's still money in your pocket!

Epilogue

SYNCHROVEST, along with one or more of the other techniques we have outlined for capital growth in this book, should result in a significant improvement in your investment results. There are advantages in some of them that have not, perhaps, been spelled out, albeit their import cannot be overlooked. To cite one example: During the course of many an investment program, the investor may come into possession of a substantial amount of "found money," a bonus, perhaps, or an inheritance. In other investment programs, he is faced with two choices: invest the money, or put it in the bank. If he invests the money, he may soon discover he has done so at a critically high juncture of the market—and he may lose a large part of it. If he banks the money, it may later develop that he has withheld this buying power from his investment program at the precise time at which it could have done the most good.

SYNCHROVEST handles this problem automatically. Excess funds can simply be deposited in the investor's *Credit Balance*—and SYNCHROVEST will decide the proper time to invest them!

For no man knoweth the top nor the bottom, nor even betwixt, nay, nor when nor why. He knoweth only *now*.

Verily, if he truly knoweth that, he knoweth all.

THE END